M000042397

FEARLESSLY MADE YOU

Surviving and Thriving
in a Perfectly Imperfect Life

FEARLESSLY MADE YOU

Surviving and Thriving
in a Perfectly Imperfect Life

Indigo River Publishing

Fearlessly Made You: Surviving and Thriving in a Perfectly Imperfect Life

Copyright © 2021 by Kristie Tobias

All rights reserved. No portion of this publication may be reproduced, stored in a retrieval system, or transmitted by any means—electronic, mechanical, photocopying, recording, or any other—except for brief quotations in printed reviews, without the prior written permission of the publisher.

Indigo River Publishing
3 West Garden Street, Suite 718
Pensacola, FL 32502
www.indigoriverpublishing.com

Editors: Mary Menke and Regina Cornell
Cover Design: Robin Vuchnich
Cover Photography: Kate Treick (front) and Phillip Makselan (back)
Interior Design: Nikkita Kent

Ordering Information: Quantity sales: Special discounts are available on quantity purchases by corporations, associations, and others. For details, contact the publisher at the address above.

Orders by U.S. trade bookstores and wholesalers: Please contact the publisher at the address above.

Printed in the United States of America

Library of Congress Control Number: 2020930216

ISBN: 978-1-950906-39-0 (paperback), 978-1-950906-45-1 (ebook)

First Edition

With Indigo River Publishing, you can always expect great books, strong voices, and meaningful messages. Most importantly, you'll always find ... words worth reading.

This book is dedicated to YOU. You have a divine purpose, a special and authentic reason for every single season in your life. You, and only you, can live out that purpose. I believe in you, and I care about you. May this book bring you closer to your fearlessly made, driven, beautiful, totally-enough-just-as-you-are self. You were made for exactly this moment in your life.

Contents

Introduction

When I started writing this book, one of the first things I was asked was, "Whom do you see out there that does what you want to do?" I remember thinking of a few authors who have great fame or even a phenomenal message. I didn't see many authors, though, who reminded me of me. The closest I could find was Michelle Obama, and though we're both black women who have muscular arms and enjoy a glass or two of wine, that's about where the comparison ends.

I know we all have a story to tell, no matter where we are in our lives. That story is hard to understand if we can't find at least one person who can not only relate to that story but also show us what it looks like to be on the other side of that story. There are stories that lift us up and bring us life, and there are stories that cause us stress, trauma, and a desire to escape from our current life. Not only do I want to show you both through my story, I also want to show you how to own your story. You may not have control over everything that happens in your life, but you can take control of how you respond, and you can thrive through even the most difficult situations. My commitment to you, the reader, is to transparently share the honest and authentic truth of who I am with the hope that you will see your story in mine.

I grew up the oldest of four in a God-fearing, high-achieving black Jamaican American middle-class family. To answer the question that undoubtedly came to mind when you saw the word *Jamaican*, yes, we grew up with delicious jerk chicken, plantains, and rice and peas (not to be confused with rice and beans; don't ever call it rice and beans in a Jamaican home—you will never be asked back!). We also ate a lot of homemade macaroni and cheese, Hamburger Helper, McDonald's, and the occasional fried chicken.

We ate all of these things not just because we were black American or Jamaican but because my family loves to eat and loves to invite people over to eat with us. Our house was a revolving door of strangers who had no place to go, colleagues of my parents, friends who had amazing home lives, and friends who were going through terrible heartache at home. My siblings and I all played sports growing up, and with every sport came a new group of friends and families that were invited to our home. We were taught that everyone has something going on in their lives, and everyone deserves to have someone to be there for them. I grew up understanding the importance of opening your home and your life to those around you.

My parents met and married before I was ever a thought and have been together "for better or for worse" for almost forty years. We have endured the excitement of a new baby; the loss of an unborn child; the thrill of new birthdays; the heartache of losing yet another young soul; the simplicity of a homemade family dinner; the chaos of misplaced anger, punched walls, and misspoken words; the exhilaration of graduation and new beginnings; and the distress of brokenness from violated trust. Through it all, I still firmly believe every family is made stronger by its dysfunction.

Living a perfectly imperfect life is our calling. There is nothing about my life that has turned out how I planned. Michael B. Jordan is still not my husband, and Channing Tatum is still not "the other man" in my life.

Student loans still dominate my life, and there are days when I consider packaged ramen noodles with cut-up chicken and vegetables a delicacy. Some days I am grateful that my plans never came to fruition, and some nights I sit on my couch or in a dark corner with a bottle of wine and question my very existence.

Too many times, I've heard people in a position of influence or leadership say a version of the same thing: "This, too, shall pass." While I appreciate the optimism, I want to rip the Band-Aid right off of this complacent statement and infuse it with a little more reality. Instead of "This, too, shall pass," how about, "This sucks a lot, and I am allowed to feel upset about it, grieve about it, and even scream about it, but I cannot wallow in it for the rest of my life"?

When I was twenty years old, I was diagnosed with post-traumatic stress disorder (PTSD). The diagnosis came after years of sexual, mental, and physical abuse from a man whom I thought I would someday marry. The concept of "This, too, shall pass" made me want to punch holes in every wall in every room. PTSD literally does not pass. It does not go away; it will always be a part of you. The same rings true for so many other disorders and diseases that, I am sure, many of you keep buried deep inside. There is no cure for these conditions, but there is a way to move forward without having them own every part of your life. It took me more than a decade to stop allowing my PTSD to sabotage my life, but within that decade, I learned a lot about what the mind, body, and spirit are capable of, both fantastically good and terrifyingly bad.

We all deserve to live a life that doesn't make us want to crawl into a hole, but sometimes it takes a little work to get there. I've spent almost twenty years working my butt off to become one of the few minority women in a leadership position as a healthcare and business consultant. For the past six years, I've spent almost 90 percent of my time traveling across the United States for work. In one week, I traveled from Florida to Ohio to Texas to Oregon to California to Georgia and back to Florida. I have accumulated fifty million SkyMiles and hotel points—this is totally an exaggeration, but it seems pretty accurate. I've made friends with all the TSA agents within most major airports, and I am a pro at fitting anyone's luggage into any overhead bin, no matter what size.

With all of my traveling and my focus on my professional growth, I have almost purposely put little effort into sustaining a viable, intimate relationship with a man. I am surrounded by great friends across the United States, and I will always find a way to grab a glass of wine with strangers or people I love at least two or three times each week. What I fail at is taking the time to invest in a relationship with a man-like person that could possibly lead to marriage with someone like Michael B. Jordan.

My all-time favorite question is, "Are you married?" immediately followed by "Do you have kids?" When I give a resounding NO to both questions, my favorite response comes next: "Oh, it's OK, dear; you have time." What does that mean—"You have time"? Am I rotting away one ovary at a time? That statement never ceases to baffle me. While I may not have chosen to be unmarried in my midthirties, I am also quite aware I would make a terrible wife right now. By the time you start reading this book, I could very well be in yet another relationship. Who knows? They happen so quickly I can't keep track. At this time in my life, I am too self-focused to commit myself to an intimate relationship.

Did you know it is OK to prioritize yourself over other people? I know—it's shocking to me, too! Do I want to be married someday? Sure, that sounds great, but I also know marriage takes work. One of the most important things I've learned in my life is it's OK to be honest with yourself about how much work you're willing to put into something—in my case, a relationship. If I know I'm not willing to put in the work, then why set myself and my partner up for failure? The effort you put into an action—in my case, dating—is equal to what you get out of it. The result: actively dating in my midthirties with some of the most, shall we say, *interesting* male candidates. My friends love living vicariously through my relationship stories because you just can't make this stuff up.

Although I have had several interesting (some may say unsuccessful) relationships, I have also had many successful ones. One of my most complex and successful relationships will always be my relationship with my faith. Growing up fully invested in the church and Christianity, I basically lived in church from when I was born until I was about eleven years old. Throughout my teens and twenties, especially after my PTSD diagnosis, my relationship with God and my faith became necessarily complex. I questioned everything from God's existence to my existence, and to be honest, I still do. I know that my God and my faith are the primary reason for the success in my life, but I also know it is important to not just take God at face value. While this is not a book on faith, it is a book on my life, and faith is part of my life.

My life can be complicated and frankly a hot mess, and if you, too, feel like your life has hot-mess tendencies, you are most definitely reading the right book! Allow me to take you on a journey of what happens when a hot mess becomes a bigger hot mess in her thirties. I'm a hard-driving corporate boss lady, sometimes unnecessarily friendly, a people pleaser, a former pageant queen, a strong black woman with OCD and plenty of insecurities, and a vulnerable woman with PTSD who refuses to let it define her. You'll laugh, you'll cry, you'll say to yourself, "If this girl can write a book, I surely can write a book," but through it all, you'll also see that, even though your life and the people in it are unpredictable, you don't have to let life own you—you can choose to own it.

ONE

The Purpose of Family

Both of my parents come from a mixed heritage. My mother grew up with a Jamaican mother, a Cuban father, and six brothers and sisters in the mountains of Jamaica and moved to Florida when she was seventeen years old. My father grew up in South Miami with a last name of Hebrew origin and a background of varied African roots and possible Native American influence. They met at the University of Florida when they were both resident advisors in the same dormitory. My favorite tale of their courtship is about when my mom would see my dad in the library asleep on top of his books, clearly using the osmosis method of studying. He claims he was "pretending" to sleep so he could scope out my mom, and my mom says he was a great actor because he was snoring.

While their actual courtship would include multiple trips to the library, disagreements during softball games, and my mom consistently falling asleep on my dad's shoulder at the movies, it was clear that they were meant to be together. To this day, their relationship is complex, messy, and always full of passion. There is absolutely nothing perfect about their marriage, but there is everything real about it. Marriage is a partnership that requires constant work. Throughout my thirty-plus years of life, they have shown me the best practices of every successful marriage, as well as the things you should never do in a relationship. At the end of the day, the complexities and lessons learned throughout their time together make me grateful that their story is my story.

They married in 1983, and both started graduate school at the University of Florida shortly after. Two years later, my mom gave birth to their prized, favorite child—that's right—me! They claim they have no favorite child, which is probably true, but as the firstborn, I was the test child. Those of you who are oldest children know exactly what I am talking about. You were the baby who was accidentally left in the grocery store because your parents weren't used to having a pint-sized mini-me by their side. You were also the baby who ate homemade baby food and wore cloth diapers for the first months of your life because your parents were so excited to have a brand-new, tiny, living human to care for.

As the firstborn, you see life unfiltered. It's just you and your parents, or parent if you grew up in a single-parent household. You see life differently because you are simply along for the ride, just like your parents.

Here is the truth about parenting: no parent knows what they are doing, especially with their first child. Back in the 1980s, there were books and tons of people with opinions about how you should parent. Nowadays, the Internet has an arsenal of "What to Do When You're Expecting" and "How to Parent Your Child without Discipline" types of websites. There is an abundance of resources out there, but my philosophy is that each parent and each child are different and therefore each parent-child relationship is unique.

There is something terrifyingly honest and beautiful about not looking to expert resources to tell you how to parent your child. When I asked my mother what type of books or advice she used when she was pregnant with and raising me and my siblings, she said simply, "I just figured it out. At the end of the day, you guys are my kids and I am your mother. God put us together for a reason, and my parenting may not be perfect, but it's mine."

While I was and still am a daddy's girl, I will always and forever be Mommy's partner in crime. I rarely left my mother's side. Because of our close relationship, I even managed to start college super early. Mom would take me to her graduate school classes when a babysitter or nanny was just not an option. We were and still are inseparable. Even with hundreds of miles physically separating us, she remains my best friend.

What I love the most about my mother is her temperament, which is the exact opposite of mine. In temperament, I truly take after my father. My mother rarely lets anything get to her. She is calm but not passive. She speaks her mind because she is a strong Jamaican woman, but she chooses her battles carefully. No matter what battle she picks, she always fights in a civilized, calm, and logical way, pointing out truths that are so honest, they hit you right in the heart.

Throughout most of my childhood, both of my parents were counselors, which means they always had a sixth sense for reading people's behavior. My mother utilized this sixth sense in a productive way. She would use what she understood about you to get to the root of what was really bothering you, in a way that had you confiding in and leaning on her as if she were the Dalai Lama. Her ease and calm are to be revered; however, if you ever push her to the point where she is no longer calm, may God have mercy on your soul, and I recommend you run as fast as you can.

I inherently take after my father in more ways than I ever did my mother. My father is a tremendously vibrant and passionate man. He loves certain people in his life the exact same way he hates some people in his life: with incredible force and vigor. When he feels strongly about something, he will steer toward it with relentless intensity. This intensity drove him to great success throughout his PhD program and his journey as a professor of counseling for over twenty years.

Like my father, I love deeply and drive relentlessly toward my goals. We both share an oftentimes intimidating intensity to always fight for what we believe to be right, even if it is polarizing to those around us. Throughout my teens and twenties, my mother taught me that choosing my battles and dialing back my intensity and passion would save me years of stress and also salvage important relationships.

The thing about passion is it can be misplaced when reactionary behavior exceeds logical thinking. I learned the consequences of reactionary behavior at five years old when a disagreement between my parents escalated into a thrown dinner plate, aggression, and horrific words from both parents. It was then that I learned how to protect myself and others. My brother, who has chosen the code name Lou, was barely three years old during this violent interaction. I remember grabbing him and running into our shared bedroom until the chaos ended. It would be the first of many chaotic nights. During such nights, I learned one main truth: people are not perfect, least of all my parents. People at their absolute worst can always be you at your absolute worst. It's an important lesson to understand how far you can actually be pushed or push yourself, to know your own breaking point.

Out of all my siblings, my sister, code name Faythe, and I took after my father's temperament. My youngest brother, code name Julius, and Lou inherited my mother's temperament.

(Sidebar: When you tell a family like mine that you're writing a book, they find a way to insert their own personalities into it. I did not ask my siblings to create code names—they created them on their own. What Lou, Faythe, and Julius have taught me is you should never take yourself or life too seriously. OK, back to the story.)

We all make the mistake of judging people, especially our parents. We find ourselves saying, "I would never make the same mistakes as my parents," or my favorite, "I will never be like them." Unintentional though they may be, these lies we tell ourselves are still lies. Inheriting flaws is as natural as inheriting positive characteristics. What's important is to learn from those flaws by asking yourself how they impact the person you are now and what you can do to compensate for or overcome these flaws.

Though every family has its failings, what I will say about my family is we truly believe family supports family, no matter what. Christmas 2018, when I went through a volatile breakup, Lou and Julius showed a side of themselves that I never knew existed—a fierce, protective side that compelled them to take care of me, no matter what. While they have always been my protective little brothers, they rarely show anger or hostility. They like to expertly navigate even the unhealthiest of relationships in a way that results in the least amount of drama, unless, as in this specific situation, they see that a stronger approach is needed. They effortlessly removed my ex-boyfriend from my life and gingerly took care of me in the months following. I received numerous phone calls, text messages, and FaceTimes from them, simply asking how I was holding up and reminding me that I was way better than the situation.

With twin personalities, my sister and I always butted heads growing up, but just like my brothers, in times of crisis, she always showed up. It took us about twenty years before we ever saw eye to eye. Strong, fierce temperaments kept us from truly understanding each other until someone dared to mess with us. It's amazing what happens when you have a baby sister. You start out as her protector, and she grows up to become yours. During that same Christmas and for months following, she showed a patient, softer side of herself. I remember her holding me that night as I did something I rarely, if ever, did in front of my siblings—cried.

You can see that the voice of my life is deeply influenced and inspired by my family. My family will intentionally and continually be a presence in my life and throughout my story. They have a voice that speaks through me when I am not strong enough to support my own voice.

I am fully aware that not everyone can be born into a family that will protect and love them no matter what. I also firmly believe family is all about whom you choose to let into your life. If you weren't fortunate enough to be born into a loving and supportive family, my challenge to you is simple: choose your family. Look around you at the people you have purposefully let into your life. Are these the people who stick with you during the calm times and during the storms? Will they stand up for you when you can't find the strength to stand up for yourself? If you answer yes to those questions, these people are your family. Love them, cherish them, and show them how much they mean to you. Don't let the stereotype of a "blood family" keep you from experiencing the camaraderie and support of a true family.

TWO

What's in an Image?

Hair is a curious thing. We all have it somewhere, and oftentimes we aren't quite sure what to do with it, especially the hair on our heads. I spent most of my life painstakingly focused on perfecting my hair. As a very young child, I learned there was a difference between my hair and the hair of some of my not-so-dark-skinned friends. For starters, as my curly-haired sisters and brothers know, not every curl behaves the same.

You may be thinking, *I bet you were adorable with that curly hair as a little girl*, and you would be absolutely right. However, adorable as I was, that hair was so hard to maintain. The braids I started out with in the morning would steadily and relentlessly evolve into a large pouf of curly madness by the end of the day.

By the time I was five years old, my mom and I both realized stronger interventions were needed to tame the unpredictability that was my ever-growing hair. Enter chemical hair straightening, also known as chemical hair relaxer. For a little hair education, chemical hair relaxer is a treatment that is placed on the hair to straighten out, or relax, the curls. It is a multi-hour-long process that typically ends with the hair relaxer recipient sitting under the hair dryer, also known as hell on earth, for hours. I distinctly remember my first chemical-relaxer hair appointment. I was terrified!

From the eyes of a child walking into a hair salon, all you see are weapons of mass hair destruction: heated straightening tools that could burn your ear if you moved the wrong way, massive guns that blew gusts of heat to simultaneously dry your hair and your eyeballs, and lots of creams that had the potential to burn your hair or your scalp if you had prolonged exposure to them.

I was always fairly small, and when I was placed in the styling chair, I had to sit in a booster seat supported by stacks of phone books. (Note: Prior to cell phones and Google, a phone book kept track of phone numbers of people and businesses in specific geographical areas throughout the United States. They were quite thick and therefore came in handy as "booster seats." If you pay close attention, you may see relics of phone books scattered throughout smaller towns where they still use phones attached to the wall.)

When I was placed in the styling chair, I was immediately sur-rounded by two stylists with big personalities and even bigger styling tools. I was a very shy and quiet child with mild separation anxiety when apart from my mother. The fear I experienced being in an unfamiliar place, having people attacking my hair while simultaneously trying to ease my anxiety was overwhelming. In retrospect, the stylists exemplified exceptional customer service, as their primary goal was to make me feel comfortable, but at the time, all I could think was this was clearly some kind of death trap.

Throughout this first of soon-to-be-many hours-long hair appoint-ments, I almost fell off the large, homemade booster seat; curiously found a way to get the chemical relaxer on my hands; and dramatically, yet quietly, cried under the aforementioned hell on earth. By the end of the appointment, I emerged a newly straight-haired five-year-old vixen.

I spent years learning the finer art of maintaining relaxed hair. There were always lots of "don'ts" concerning my hair: I couldn't wear it in a ponytail for too long because it would damage my chemically treated, already-fragile tresses. I couldn't wear it pulled back from my face too tightly, mainly because it made me look permanently surprised and like I had a monster forehead; and I couldn't work out or swim (not that I enjoyed swimming, but the option was nice) within forty-eight hours of getting my relaxer because I would damage the newly straightened locks, which would revert to a warped and twisted version of my curly hair. Oh, and let's not forget, these salon trips were expensive, like choose-whether-you-eat-this-week-or-get-your-hair-done expensive. For those of you who haven't spent much time in a salon, you're probably thinking, *This sounds horrid! Why do this to yourself?* It all falls under one very important word that would have a continuous impact on my life: *image.*

We live in a time where "natural," non-chemically-treated, hair and makeup-free Mondays are celebrated. This wasn't the case in the nineties and early 2000s. Instead, we focused on stick-straight, nontextured hair, and perfect makeup. By the time I hit my teens, in the late nineties, I was no more adept at understanding my relaxed hair than I was at five years old.

I was an active and athletic child, and I just let my mom tell me how to handle my hair. Because I was so involved in sports, I spent a lot of time as the only girl among the boys. My baby sister is nine years my junior, with my two brothers sandwiched in between. It was always me and my two brothers. The more boyish, athletic environment did not contribute to any comprehension of how to fix my hair or have a more ladylike image.

By the time I was twelve years old, one of my beloved middle school teachers noticed that, while physically I was becoming a stereotypical young lady, my behavior more closely resembled that of a young boy. In 1997, unless you were aiming to become a professional athlete, it was expected that you would eventually grow out of the tomboy stage and start to present yourself to the world as a young lady. My teacher talked with my mom about entering me into a contest that would help me become more ladylike. This contest was a beauty pageant with several divisions, including a pre-teen division.

Now, before you start reeling and saying, "How could your mother even consider entering you into a pageant?" let me stop you with some truth: My mother is my role model and best friend. When people ask whom I would want to emulate, 100 percent of the time I say my mother. I learned decades later that my mother grew up not believing she was beautiful or even feeling very confident in herself. She never wanted me to feel that way, and she also never wanted me to face any barriers to success. At the time, she rightfully saw the pageant industry as an opportunity for me to grow and thrive in a world where my image could lead me to great success.

I entered my first pageant at twelve years old, but the preparation for the pageant—well, let's just say I quickly learned what kind of lady I was *not*. I had to learn to walk in little kitten heels that felt like six-inch stilettos, put on an evening gown as opposed to softball pants and a T-shirt, perfect my silky straightened hair and ladylike makeup, and the best part—I had to come up with a talent. At the time, the only talent that I had besides playing softball was playing the clarinet, which we were quickly told was not the type of talent that would make me successful at the pageant. The pageant gurus had also never heard my version of "Under the Sea" from *The Little Mermaid,* so they were clearly unaware of my amazing skills. Regardless, I needed a more suitable talent.

My mother is truly a genius. She came up with a perfect talent that would make a far greater statement than I could understand at the time. I would perform a dramatic monologue of Sojourner Truth's famous speech, "Ain't I a Woman."

Now, it's time for a little 1800s female-empowerment education: Sojourner Truth, or Isabella Baumfree (her given name), was one of the fiercest advocates for women's rights. She lived a horrifically violent and painful life as a slave until she escaped to freedom in 1826. She was one of the key female drivers of the women's suffrage movement, an abolitionist, an evangelist, and an author. Her famous speech, "Ain't I a Woman," launched her journey as an equal rights activist walking alongside other powerful activists, such as Frederick Douglass.

My image was questioned during this talent performance because, instead of wearing a sparkly gown like the singers or a sassy, skimpy costume like the dancers, I wore a borrowed, old 1800s-style dress typical of those worn by female slaves. The genius behind this decision was subtle. My mother identified very early on that you had to "play the game" to get into the system, but once in the system, you make your own rules.

I went on to win every award, including Best Talent, at that pageant, except for the actual pageant queen title. The winner of that title was a fair-skinned, blonde-haired, blue-eyed schoolmate, who we later found out won the title but no other awards. This was the first of many pageants where my image and appearance were good enough to earn me the highest accolades, but not good enough for me to win a major honor, like representing my city, town, or state as a not-so-fair-skinned pageant queen.

Competing in pageants in the state of North Carolina opened my eyes to a lot of expectations around what was considered the appropriate image in the South. I went on to compete in pageants throughout my teens and twenties, and rarely saw any teenagers or women who looked like me. For the handful of us who happened to be nonwhite, we had an unspoken respect and camaraderie that developed into a sisterhood, which we still maintain twenty years later. What I learned was, while people want to own the image they use to show others what beauty and success should look like, I have a responsibility to own what I allow my image to stand for and how I choose to project that image.

While it is absolutely true that your substance as a person is not defined by your external looks, this is not the type of book that tells you, "Don't worry about your outward appearance; it's what is on the inside that matters." We are human and imperfect. We were never called to be perfect, but I do believe we have a responsibility to be honest and authentic. I take a lot of pride in my image. When it comes to image, it is so much more than outward appearance; it is how you present yourself.

For too long, I allowed certain physical attributes, like my hair, to keep me from expressing my inner self. The image others had of me became more important than the image I had of myself. I had to literally break down my physical barriers and break up with the art of perfection. I broke up with the concept that there was one way to look in the world to be successful. To bring this full circle, by the time I reached my thirties, I finally realized I had ownership over something that had bound me to an accepted but not authentic image of myself—my hair. At about thirty-one, I decided to take the "natural" hair journey and break up with the chemicals that straightened my hair. To take that a step farther, by thirty-three I cut all of my hair off and rocked a bright-blonde mohawk, and at this very moment I rock a sassy platinum or sometimes dark-silver finger wave in hair that is much shorter than most men's. My image is no longer imprisoned by this need to portray what people expect from me.

You have the freedom not only to care about your own personal expression but also to own your personal expression. I encourage you to ask yourself what it is that you want to say. You also have the freedom not to spend hundreds of thousands of dollars on your hair, makeup, or other products to build an image that, in the end, is not a true reflection of you. Ultimately, you should be empowered to be whom you want to be and to allow your image to express that.

My challenge to you: instead of letting other people—family, friends, spouses, or even social media comparisons—own the image you are reflecting, take one step today to adapt your image to truly reflect the person you want to own. At no point would anyone say this is an easy task, so take it one baby step at a time. If, like me, you are on the shorter side and regularly wear heels to appear taller, maybe buy yourself a pair of lower heels, or even flats. One day a week, don't just wear those flats, own those flats.

You may find yourself branching out even further, from owning flats to owning a new hairstyle to eventually digging deeper and owning a more confident way to stand up for yourself. By the end of the year, you may find yourself transitioning from wearing flats to negotiating your own professional self-worth in a business meeting. While starting small with flats or a bolder hairstyle may seem simple and trivial, it takes you one step closer to allowing yourself to own your inner badass.

Owning your image is a dynamic journey. I constantly struggle with ensuring I am reflecting someone I am proud of, but the journey and the challenge I give myself every day to stand up for myself is absolutely worth every doubt and fear in my mind. Others may look at me and say, *Well, that's not how I would choose to live my life*, or *Wow! Good for her for thinking she can pull off that hair*, but I find joy and empowerment in knowing that those people are not me, and they have no ownership of my life. Only I can own the person that I want reflected in my actions, in my words, and, yes, even in my hair.

Take pride and strength in knowing you are the only you that will ever live, and let your image reflect that strength.

THREE

The Bond of Shared Experiences

During my travels, one of the most complex questions I receive on almost a daily basis is, "Where do you live?" My answer is simple: "I have no earthly idea."

For the past six years, I have spent my professional career traveling the United States four to five days out of each week. I spend more time in seat 11D on an airplane than I do in my own bed. Most days I have no idea if it's Monday or Friday. I have a dear friend, we shall call her my "partner in wine," who is my Friday alarm clock, especially when I am in my home in Pensacola, Florida. At about three p.m. every Friday, I receive the classic text message, "Wine tonight?" That's my reminder of two very important things: (1) I am home in Pensacola, and (2) it's Friday, or as I like to call it, Wine-Day.

While I love to travel, I never flew until I was twenty years old. My first flight was to Moscow, Russia. After a rigorous application and interviewing process, I was selected as one of ten students at my undergraduate school, Wake Forest University, to serve as a Helping Hands Delegate to Russia. The program would have us living in and building an orphanage, or children's home as it was called in Russia, for two weeks. It was an opportunity of a lifetime.

While the Helping Hands program included a scholarship that covered about 50 percent of the cost of the trip, program activities, and excursions, the other 50 percent was the responsibility of each participant to cover. The additional cost would total around $2,500. For most of my classmates, their parents were able to cover those funds. That was not, nor would it ever be, an option for me.

When I was seventeen years old, and about one month after I submitted my acceptance letter to Wake Forest University (a $50,000-per-year private university), both of my parents lost their jobs. At the time, my mother was a vice principal at my high school, and my father was a professor of counseling at a state university. These losses would devastate not only my family but our community as well. Injustice and scandal would surround both of my parents' jobs, and the existence of unfair circumstances would become very real for my family. Within six months of my mother losing her job and after several applications and interviews, she would regain employment as a vice principal in another county. My father would never go back into the education system, at least not as a professor. Moving forward, the support of my family would fall to my mother and me.

We didn't have fifty extra dollars for this trip, much less $2,500. I quickly learned the art of humility, grace, and self-fundraising. With the help of my mother's family, friends of my parents, and friends of their friends who believed in me, as well as the extensive, eloquently written fundraising letters I sent out, I raised close to $3,000 to support my trip. Many well-thought-out Russian trinkets were bought as thank-you gifts for the wonderful group of people who believed in me in a way that I never realized was possible.

In the months leading up to the trip, we semisuccessfully learned the Russian language and customs, and specific dos and don'ts of our trip. I would be one of two minorities, and in Russia, the distinction between Russian and non-Russian was very important. My classmate was of dark-skinned Asian descent, and we received a few more specific instructions based on race relations.

Russia is a collectivistic society. They take care of their own, and if you are an outsider, they are incredibly cautious until they understand more about your purpose in their country. By comparison, America is an individualistic society. Individuals choose whether to let you into their group based on their own individual cultural backgrounds. Because of the collectivistic mind-set of the Russians, my classmate and I stood out distinctly as not being Russian. We were directed not to take offense at this and to understand we might need to be patient with people who might not be immediately receptive to us.

In May of 2002, when we landed in Moscow, the first place we visited was Red Square, which is considered the central point of Moscow. It's where all the city's major streets intersect. Understanding that I was in a new country with a limited understanding of the language and where my skin color would already stand out in a sea of very fair-skinned people, I knew I should be more aware and conscious of my image. As we walked off of our large passenger van and into Red Square, I noticed an elderly, seemingly inebriated Russian man walking briskly in the direction of our group. Without warning, he grabbed my face, kissed me square on the lips, and yelled "Goddess!" then went off on his merry way. I felt extremely welcomed to Russia!

Throughout my time in Russia, I was greeted in two opposing ways. I was either treated as a goddess and fawned over, mainly by older Russian men, or I was ostracized and eye contact was avoided.

While our main purpose in Russia was to rebuild the Moscow Children's Home, we were also challenged to immerse ourselves in the Russian culture. As part of that immersion, we were asked to be special guests at an underground English social club. While I don't know if it was intentionally a secretive club, it was literally several feet under the city. This club was composed of various Russian people who wished to become fluent in the English language. We were asked to be guest speakers and talk about our experience, as well as help explain America and some of the finer points of the English language.

When we first arrived, it was a social hour, and every single one of my classmates, including my other minority friend, was quickly pulled into conversation among a sea of Russians. I was left by myself in the middle of a room surrounded by people deliberately not talking to me. While I have always been taught to be independent and comfortable holding my own, this stark aloneness was extremely disconcerting. So I did what I usually do when I feel uncomfortable—I found the food table. While at the food table, I ran into the man who would later become my first Russian friend during our time at the club. When he greeted me, the first words out of his mouth were, "So, do you want to know why no one is talking to you?" to which I responded, "Oh, it's because I'm black."

Between bites of cheese and crackers, he explained that while my skin color was outwardly a difference, the reason people weren't talking to me was they didn't know what to think of me. He shared that, in Russian culture, the only thing they knew about black American women was that they were video girls in rap videos. When everyone saw this twenty-year-old, fully dressed, not-voluptuous black American woman, they were confused and did not know how to respond, so they just pretended I wasn't there until they could figure it out. I've never been more relieved to be ostracized because I was not a video girl!

While we were at the English social club, one of the requests was that all ten of us Helping Hands delegates take the stage and speak to the group about our experiences. As a natural public speaker and a communication major, this type of opportunity would usually excite me. Given the nongreeting I received, though, I quickly asked my new Russian friend for his advice. He said, "Go last so you are the first person people remember, and be exactly the person you have been with me." During our conversations, we had exchanged hilariously sarcastic banter and spent most of our time laughing about the ridiculousness of me not being a video girl. He encouraged me to just be authentic and honest and let everything else play out.

I anxiously took his advice, and when it was my turn to close out the speaking, the first thing I said was, "Well, I guess I stick out like a sore thumb." The very Russian, very quiet room erupted in laughter, and it was then I knew I was destined to be a comedian. Lies—this is not that kind of book! It was then I realized I was going to make it out of this place talking to at least one more Russian.

After I finished what would be a speech filled with lots of laughter, I walked off the stage with my head down and my eyes almost completely closed. While I knew everyone found me entertaining, I was still nervous they wouldn't talk to me. When I finally made my way back to the main floor, I lifted my head and almost ran smack into over seventy new Russian friends. I spent the next hour excitedly conversing in English and Russian with almost everyone at the club. I was inundated with questions about my life and my background. People were genuinely interested in the non-video-girl black American.

Before leaving, I found my original Russian friend in the back of the room. We made quick eye contact, exchanged a wink and a head nod, and both disappeared back into the crowd as if we had never met.

While the English social club was a great initiation into Russian culture, we were still there for a very important, more challenging reason: to rebuild the Moscow Children's Home. We spent eight to ten hours each day climbing up rickety scaffolding and scraping potentially lead-based paint from the orphanage walls and ceilings. We would listen to Dane Cook and laugh boisterously, while I'm sure the Russian contractors who were hired to help us found us unamusing. A friend who later became my boyfriend (at least for a couple of months), who was also on this trip and fluent in Russian, would later tell us the not-so-pleasant words the contractor used to describe the seemingly inept American kids during our first couple of days of work. By the end of our two weeks, this same contractor would embrace us and, in Russian, tell us how much he appreciated us.

While our main priority was rebuilding the orphanage, we also had the opportunity to bond with the children who lived in the orphanage. We would delay our work so we could spend time playing with the children or just talking to them in our broken, inconsistent Russian.

Children's homes in Russia were not solely for children without parents. Due to the economy, it was difficult for parents to care for their children during the week. Most parents would drop off their children on Sunday or Monday, and their children would stay at the orphanage until the weekend. Friday pickup days were always bittersweet. The children with families were always super excited the whole day because they knew they would get to see their parents. The children who did not have families to pick them up would be reserved and unemotional, as they were used to this Friday exchange. We found it important to bond with and distract those children even more on pickup days.

I befriended two young Russian teenage girls who were part of the crew of children that were usually not picked up on the weekends. They were very tough yet vulnerable. We would talk about life, and I learned that we shared an unfortunate similar background of sexual assault. While my goal during my trip was to ignore the PTSD from that abusive experience, I found myself forced to deal with the emotions that came from that violation. These two girls taught me that though language or culture may separate people, experiences will always bring us together. These girls and I shared a bond that only those who have survived sexual assault can share. We sealed that bond by exchanging handmade friendship bracelets. I keep mine in a Russian jewelry box as a reminder that I will never be alone in this journey.

Now, as you are reading this chapter, I know the biggest question in your mind is, "So you were in Russia; talk to us about the vodka." OK, friends, allow me to step away from the original story for a brief tale about the realities of Russian vodka.

During 2002, Russia had one of the highest rates of alcoholism and alcohol-related suicide; however, there is a big difference in the way Russians drink and the way Americans drink. Russians drink discreetly and subtly, and you could rarely tell if they were drunk (except for my elderly man-friend in Red Square). It was deeply frowned upon to appear drunk in public. Americans, on the other hand . . . well, have you ever been to a bar during happy hour or, better yet, any type of major sporting event? Public drunkenness is somewhat the norm, especially in the world of a college student.

At night, after we finished our manual labor for the day, we visited restaurants, bars, and karaoke rooms, and of course, sampled the Russian vodka. I was only two weeks shy of my twenty-first birthday, and up until that point my experience with alcohol was extremely limited. I grew up in a family that did not drink. My mom's father (whom I loved dearly) was an alcoholic until he passed. Because of this, other than cooking sherry, we never had alcohol in the house. I quickly learned that when you request a shot of vodka in Russia, one shot is actually two shots. Needless to say, we experienced some public drunkenness. We were more of the talk-and-laugh-too-loud type of drunks, so while annoying, we were harmless.

We learned a lot about Russian drinking culture, especially during our last day working in the Moscow Children's Home. It is customary to celebrate benefactors with a farewell dinner. The dinner includes one 750 mL bottle of wine and one-fifth of vodka per every four people. During our farewell dinner, our two adult chaperones and two Russian hosts sat at the head of the table, leaving our group of ten at the end of the table to enthusiastically pour our own drinks. We were not aware of one Russian custom: that shots of vodka were used for toasts. In America, we typically toast with champagne or wine, so we were liberally pouring ourselves shot after shot of vodka. About an hour or two into the dinner, the hosts stood up and declared it was time to toast. In our group of ten, we had three almost-empty fifths of vodka. Our toasts were sloppy, tear filled, and, let's just be honest, hilarious. Our two adult chaperones tried to be upset with us, but even they couldn't help laughing at the group of drunken twenty-year-olds who couldn't handle their Russian vodka.

Russia will always hold a special place in my heart, even with the political drama of this current presidency. Culturally, I learned how to bond with people based on their experiences. I learned the simple art of listening and observing the people around me to better understand who they are and not just what they look like. My vulnerability and in-securities were constantly tested, but those tests opened me up to a way of thinking that wouldn't have been possible without the bond I shared with my first Russian friend and the two beautiful teenage girls who shared my story.

As you approach new environments and situations, allow your discomfort with the unknown to push you to connect with a new soul. Engage with someone in a different way because of your discomfort. Learn what life looks like through their eyes, and use that learning to open yourself up to a new way of thinking and understanding. Take it from a woman who was considered a goddess, a video girl, and finally a friend in a foreign country: you will never regret taking the chance to vulnerably connect with someone else.

FOUR

It's Not Your Fault

***Disclaimer: The content of this chapter is heavy and deep. It's the story that led up to my PTSD. It's a story that I know so many women share and so many never get to tell. May my story give you the strength and empowerment to survive and thrive through your story.*

When I was about twelve years old, I kissed my first boy. It was a magical experience for both of us.

My soon-to-be boyfriend had been eyeing me throughout the day. When he finally mustered the courage to talk to me, he asked me one simple question: "Can I walk you to your bus after school?" Of course, I excitedly and nervously said, "Yes!" I had no way of anticipating the moment we would share next. I don't remember anything that happened in school that day because I was impatiently waiting for the clock to strike 3:30 p.m., the end of our school day.

By the time I walked to the school exit, he was already waiting, anxiously searching for me. When our eyes met, we both smiled goofily and giggled. He reached for my hand, and we walked slowly toward our respective buses. We arrived at my bus, and he gently pulled me to the side, so we were slightly hidden between the lines of buses. He pulled me closer for what I thought was a hug, but instead he gathered his twelve-year-old-boy nerves and leaned directly in for a kiss. It was an actual lips-met, tongues-found-each-other bona fide French kiss. My friends who were already in their seats had their faces pressed to the window, and when I finally made my way onto the bus, they swarmed me, wanting to know all the juicy details. From that moment, it was clear to both of us and anyone who saw that romantic kiss that we were an item.

Our relationship was love at first sight, although really it was more a game of passing notes and hearing from our friends that we had a crush on each other. For a twelve-year-old boy, he was very good looking. He reminded me of what the members of Boys II Men looked like when they were only Boys II Boys. We would have a one-month affair that ended shortly after I contracted mononucleosis. At that time, it was not known as the "kissing disease," and besides, the only boy I had kissed was my Boys II Boys–look-alike boyfriend. I contracted it from lots of stress and just being a kid.

Valentine's Day fell during the two weeks I was out sick, and I learned that my boyfriend had been waiting for me in the bus parking lot with flowers, balloons, and a beautiful Bath and Body Works gift set. To this day, that is still one of the most romantic Valentine's gifts I never received. Sadly, he didn't know I was out sick, and when my friends broke the news, they said he was devastated. Our relationship lasted maybe a week after I finally returned to school. I should have learned how every woman should be treated by my Boys II Boys boyfriend. He was romantic, kind to everyone around me, respectful to my family, and he valued twelve-year-old, driven, and ambitiously focused me.

I went on to date actively throughout my middle and high school years. Not much has changed since then, except I am intentionally working on being more discerning about the men in my life now than I was in middle school.

Growing up, I was really good at following the rules, and I was always the "good girl." I was good at doing the right things, making the best grades, being student body president and varsity cheerleading captain—all with a focus on setting myself up for success for college and my future. Even in my teens, I was driven and focused on professional development and growth. I was always incredibly responsible, a true stereotypical oldest child with the weight of the world on her shoulders.

My personal life proved to be a little different. Because I was so focused on being "good" all the time, I wanted to act out. I wanted to try new things that my friends weren't doing. I wanted to live a life outside of my own shadow.

With that knowledge in hand, it should come as no surprise that I decided to experiment with certain aspects of life a lot sooner than some of my friends. From twelve years old on, boys were always interested in me, and I became very interested in the attention they were giving me. I was fully developed by this time, and though I didn't have a lot of curves, I had enough to intrigue boys my age as well as men much older than me. Although we grew up in a strict, faith-focused household where things like sexual intercourse were reserved for marriage, by the time I was fourteen years old, I was steadily rebelling against the traditional mindset of my parents.

During the early summer of 2000, I lost my virginity in the girls' bathroom at my high school. We were in drivers' education class, and I was sitting next to a friend of mine who I knew was sexually attracted to me. He found any reason he could to touch me during class, and I did absolutely nothing to stop him. By the time class was over, we were both sexually on edge, and when I went to the back of the school, to the girl's bathroom, he followed me. While I'd had lots of make-out sessions in my brief fourteen years of life, and an unwanted sexual encounter with a now-estranged relative, I had absolutely no experience with actual penis-to-vagina sex.

We were mostly clothed and standing in the last bathroom stall. It was cold, uncomfortable, and quick. I didn't really know what to do with my hands or my body, but he had no problem doing what he needed to do to get the result he wanted. I went into that bathroom with no expectations and walked out of that bathroom slightly disheartened and no longer a virgin.

He would be the first of several awkward sexual encounters. I liked the idea of sex, but I was in no way mature enough to attach emotional connection or meaning to it. What I did find was, though I wasn't sure what I was doing, most of the guys I was with knew even less about what they were doing.

Sex became an outlet, a way for me to do something most of my friends were not doing, and be good at it. I enjoyed the control behind it. I started to learn what boys and men liked, and I felt empowered that I could own the sexual experience. I was always safe, making sure any guy I was with "wrapped it up," and by the time I was sixteen and my parents found out I was having sex, I was also on birth control. While I will always have mixed feelings about how early I started having sex, and though my parents would have preferred I waited until I was more mature, they did teach us about safe sex and how to take care of ourselves.

While my close friends in high school knew about my sex life, other students may have heard rumblings but typically just ignored it. My "good girl" reputation for the most part preceded my reputation as being sexually experienced. I did hear accounts from one or two of my partners who couldn't keep our experience to themselves. That was the main reason I stopped dating guys in high school. Their immaturity and big mouths started to impact the image I wanted people to have of me. So I found a new outlet to connect with people, more specifically, men.

During this same time period, my friends and I were all introduced to something very powerful: the computer and dial-up Internet. In 1999, AOL and online chat rooms were all the rage. My best friends and I would spend hours, mainly at night, talking to each other in chat rooms or via AOL Instant Messenger. Cell phones were rare, and our version of the art of text messaging was writing a note on a piece of paper and giving it to a friend during class. This new foray into computer life would open amazing and dangerous opportunities.

AOL chat room introductions always included three key letters—A, S, L: age, sex, location—especially if you were trying to find a new love interest. My girlfriends and I would set a time to meet up online in certain chat rooms. We would connect with guys via the chat room; then if we received the coveted, "Can we talk outside of the chat room?" request, we would start private conversations with the guys we met. For the most part, it was harmless. There was an understood rule that we could have conversations and even exchange personal information, but we wouldn't meet any of these guys. Some of them went to neighboring high schools, so we may have hinted at seeing each other at school events; but for the most part, they were just flirtatious strangers on the Internet—with one exception.

As with the other flirtatious strangers, the exception and I met in a chat room, and we agreed to have a private conversation outside of the room. We talked privately on AOL almost every night for about a month. We exchanged phone numbers with the understanding that he would never call me unless we were certain no one else would answer the phone. He said he was ten years older than me, which, at fourteen years old, was intriguing and dangerous. He was a professor at a local college, and I thought that was attractive. He was a grown man with an entire life, which just increased the attraction.

I didn't question his being a twenty-four-year-old professor until much later in the relationship. Even when we transitioned to phone conversations, we still talked every night. We talked for at least a month before we had our first disagreement, and he said, "So, does this mean we're broken up?" As a teenager, I didn't see the manipulation in that statement. We had never "determined the relationship," which he, of course, knew. The best way to draw someone in is to threaten them with taking one's attention way. We became a couple without ever having seen each other, but he didn't want to go much longer without meeting in person.

We planned our meeting to be on the same night that one of my best friends was spending the night. The house my family lived in throughout my high school years was next to the town softball field, on a small back road that was closeted deep in the forest by large trees, making it almost impossible to see anyone driving down it. By now, I was fifteen and excited to meet my boyfriend for the first time. My best friend was less than excited, as she reminded me about the dangers of meeting "psychos" on the Internet. While I was slightly nervous about that, I was more intrigued by my relationship with an older man and this secretive meeting.

After everyone was asleep, my best friend and I snuck out of the house. We ran quickly into the forest to wait for the car. Once we saw it, she stayed back in the woods, while I approached and got into the car. What we didn't see coming was that he would drive off, leaving my best friend in the woods.

Prior to this rendezvous, my friends who knew about my boyfriend, including my best friend who was with me that night, were not happy nor supportive of our relationship, much less us meeting. They instinctively knew something was off with my new boyfriend, and while I didn't disagree with them, I was at that stubborn, invincible stage of my life where I wasn't concerned with other people's opinions or instincts.

When he drove off, I immediately panicked, knowing if I was gone for longer than ten minutes, my best friend would alert my parents. As he was driving, I tried to convince him to turn around by telling him that my best friend was still in the woods by herself. He didn't even feign interest or concern. It was when I told him she would probably run and tell my parents, who would immediately come and find me, that he reluctantly turned around and returned to the small, forested back road.

I don't know where he would have taken me that night. I don't know if it would have been back to his place or somewhere else, but I knew I wanted to get out of the car. When we stopped in front of my friend—I was grateful she was still waiting in the woods—I tried to get out of the car, but he locked the doors and grabbed my arms. He didn't even glance at my friend, who was anxiously waiting mere feet from the car. He explained that he hadn't come this far for me to just leave after seeing him for five minutes and that I owed him something more. It was the first of many times that he would remind me of what I owed him.

I was used to being in control of my sexual encounters. Now, though, I was not only not in control, but I had no desire to engage in any type of sexual activity. I was scared because I didn't know this man in the car with me who claimed to be my boyfriend. I didn't like the way he was looking at me or how he grabbed my arms. Instinctively, I tried to turn toward the car door, searching for my friend, who had now disappeared unnoticed into the woods. Panicked that she was going to tell my parents, anxiety and fear set in. At the time, I wasn't sure if I wanted my parents to come rescue me or not, but regardless, I knew if they found out I would be in more trouble than I could imagine.

He pulled me in to kiss me and touch me in ways that I hadn't been touched. Everywhere he touched me hurt. It wasn't the fun, flirtatious way I had been touched by the other boys and men in my life; this was a possessive groping that made me feel owned, not cared for. I was deathly silent. I wasn't sure how to respond or how to get out of the car. It felt like hours since I had seen my friend, but really it was merely minutes. My body had frozen, and I was so confused, leaving or fighting back seemed foreign. He grabbed my head and held it down until I gave him oral sex. It was the only time I fought, and the pain I felt on the back of my head stopped me from fighting further. Once he was satisfied, he pulled my head up by the hair and kissed me on the cheek. He told me I could go, and he would call me the next day.

When I got out of the car, he quickly drove away and I started running toward the house. I almost barreled into my best friend, who was hiding behind a tree deep in the woods. I told her I was scared she had left me to tell my parents, and she said that something in her told her to stay with me. She asked me what had happened in the car, and I told her I didn't want to talk about it, that I just wanted to get inside. We walked back to the house in silence, a heaviness weighing on both of us that we wouldn't discuss until years later.

That night would shape my boyfriend and my on-again, off-again relationship for six years. I wouldn't reveal what happened in that car for years. I felt vulnerable and violated but also confused because it was my first "grown-up" relationship. I thought I understood sex and sexual activity, but what we did couldn't be defined as any of that. As you're reading this, I'm sure you feel like I do in writing this, like it's a horror movie and you want to tell the girl to run away and save herself.

Unfortunately, I wouldn't run away; I would actually grow even more intimate with him. We would meet in clandestine locations. Trips to the mall with my friends would really be everyone meeting at the mall and me being dropped off to get in the car with my boyfriend and go back to his place. Every single one of my friends hated him with a passion. They would never spend more than five seconds with him, typically during the pickup and drop-off at the mall, but they didn't like the answers I gave when they asked me about our relationship.

While we did talk, a lot of our relationship was physical, and I learned (taught by him) to be more comfortable with his sexual style, which can only be described as forceful. Although the relationship was messy at best, I appreciated being in another world when I was with him. I enjoyed being together, just the two of us. We absolutely never left his couch or his bedroom, much less his house. He talked to me like an equal, not like a high school kid. We talked vaguely about his work as a college music professor and what he was teaching his students. I told him about my plans for college. At the time, I was entertaining the idea of moving away to college or at least to another city, which, on reflection, was not something he wanted. While he had moments when he was kind and sweet to me, he was also controlling and sadistic.

By the end of my junior year in high school, I ended the relationship. At the time, I thought it was for good. We talked on and off through-out my senior year, but by the time I graduated, I cut off all communication. I didn't hear from him again until the fall of my junior year at Wake Forest.

By then, I had been in and out of serious and casual relationships, but none with the intensity and danger of that relationship. He emailed me through my AOL account and apologized for his behavior when we were together. During our time together, his controlling tendencies had hurt me physically, emotionally, and sexually. He scared me more often than I wanted to admit, but I was still uncontrollably drawn to him. I thought I was in love. In his email, he not only apologized for the pain he put me through, but he also said the reason he hurt me was because he loved me, and he wanted to marry me. He wanted me to be the one, and the feelings he felt for me scared him, so he hurt me to push me away.

I was in a committed relationship when he emailed me. The man I was with was one of the main reasons I had stopped talking to my ex-boyfriend. While I told my current boyfriend about the email, I allowed him to believe I was just going to ignore it and move on.

I was living in one of the dormitories at my university with nine girlfriends. They knew about my ex-boyfriend and, like everyone else, despised him. He and I started secretly seeing each other. He would pick me up at my dorm, and I would spend evenings at his place. Depending on his mood, he would drop me back off that same night, especially if we had a disagreement.

On one such night, I began to realize how fearful I was of him. I was irritated because I had a lot of schoolwork to get done, and I was always on edge because I knew I shouldn't be around him. I had lied to my current boyfriend about where I was, and I was trying to keep things as nonsexual as possible between us. My ex always got a thrill out of pushing my buttons, so he started touching me, and I resisted. I didn't resist much, but I just wasn't in the mood to deal with him. He pinned me down, laughed, and wouldn't let me up until he got what he wanted. I was frustrated and upset, and I mumbled afterward, "Can you take me back?" He looked me dead in the eyes and yelled, "I will take you back when I'm ready, not when you're ready." The snap caught me off guard, and when he walked by me and I flinched, he turned around, sneered at me, and said, "Don't flinch when I'm near you." At that point, his words and sexual dominance were what kept me in my place. Now I was older and more assertive, and he was losing his patience with me.

It was a couple of weeks before I saw him again, and that would be the last night we were together. We were having a huge on-campus party among our fraternities and sororities. I used the excitement of my friends to hide the fact that although I was going out, I wasn't going out with them. One of my best girlfriends and sorority sisters, who is still both to me, caught on to the fact that I was trying to see my ex-boyfriend. She cornered me and told me it was a bad idea and that she couldn't let me go. I told her she was probably right, but when she stepped away and went back to the excitement in our dorm, I ran out of the dorm to his car.

With the fear I had from our previous night together, I wanted to take the edge off. I wasn't much of a drinker, but I knew enough to know that a little bit of alcohol calmed me. He had Absolut lemon vodka, a drink that to this day I still can't look at. That night, I had ten shots of vodka spaced throughout at least four hours. I didn't feel right, so I wanted the vodka to numb the increasing fear I had being there that night. When I told him I didn't feel very well, he put his arms around me, kissed me, and said, "It's OK, baby. I've got you." He repeated that to me as he led me to his bedroom. The room spun, and I told him, "I don't know what's going on. I don't want to do this." And again he said, "It's OK, baby. I've got you."

I blacked out and woke up naked on his bed. Opening my eyes, I saw him standing next to me. I knew if I resisted, I would risk his anger from the previous night, so I told him to please use protection. I blacked out again and woke up to him getting on the bed. My instincts kicked in, and I realized everything was all wrong, that nothing about what was happening was right, and I was terrified that he was going to do something to me that could never be taken back.

I opened my eyes and yelled, "No! This can't happen!" and tried to get off the bed. I was immediately slammed back down, and his entire body weight covered me. I kicked and screamed and pushed, but he didn't even look at me, just forced himself into me. I turned my head to stare blindly at the white wall until he was finished. Naively thinking now that he got what he wanted, we were done, I tried to get up again, and he slammed me back down. He told me I wasn't going anywhere and to not make him hurt me. I made the mistake of saying he wouldn't hurt me, thinking it would appeal to the kindness he sometimes showed. As he slapped me across the face once, and then twice, I knew things were different. Immediately following the slaps, he raped me again. I didn't scream; I didn't struggle. I cried and told him no. When I looked him in the eyes, I saw nothing. There was no emotion. Whether it was true or not, I felt a sickening fear that if I stayed there, he would hurt me worse or even kill me.

When he rolled off of me, I curled myself into the fetal position to strategically face the opening of the bedroom. My body was in searing pain, but I knew I had to leave. I knew if I ran, I could make it out of the bedroom.

As I was desperately trying to build up the courage to run, he pinned me facedown on the bed. When he entered me this time, he drew blood, and my scream was so full of pain that he fell back toward the opening of the bedroom door. The bathroom opening was closer than the door to the bedroom, so I ran there and locked the door. I knew I had one shot to leave, to take advantage of the shock that I saw on his face. I didn't stay in the bathroom for longer than ten minutes, and when I opened the door he was on the other side of the bedroom. I bolted, completely naked, toward the stairs that would lead me outside. I grabbed my cell phone and speed-dialed my boyfriend to tell him where I was. I barely got one word out before my ex came after me and knocked the phone out of my hand. I fled through the door to the neighbor's house and banged on the door until they let me in.

The police would later tell me that when the neighbors saw me, they were scared until they saw the marks on my face, and they knew something was wrong. They took me in, covered me up in a pair of shorts and a T-shirt, and held me until the police and crime scene investigators arrived. My ex-boyfriend, not one to ever lose face, would pick up my abandoned cell phone and tell my current boyfriend that I went crazy, running out of the house naked and drunk. He actually gave my boyfriend directions to come get me, as he had no idea the police were on their way. My boyfriend, two of my best friends, and the rape-and-trauma advocate from my university arrived at the same time as the ambulance, and they all followed me to the hospital. My current boyfriend, though hurt, knew my sordid history with my ex-boyfriend and had to be detained by the police for fear that he would kill my ex.

During the ambulance ride, I found myself at peace. There was a feeling of relief that I was ending a chapter in my life that had kept me captive for six years. Getting over my ex-boyfriend was never an option. He had a hold and a pull on me that is unfortunately common in most abusive relationships. The pull is manipulation and power.

His power was more sordid than I ever knew. The police report revealed that he wasn't only sadistic, he was a potential pedophile. Throughout our relationship, he got angry if I ever questioned how old he was. The police report explained why: though he said he was ten years older than I was, he was actually twenty years older.

The pain from the lies would complicate my understanding of the relationship for years to come. Knowing he was a terrible person wouldn't keep me from believing I was at least partly responsible for his abusive behavior during the six years we were together. I made plenty of mistakes, but I will say this now with strength and conviction: this was not my fault, and if you're in an abusive situation, it is not your fault. My ex-boyfriend made a choice to rape, assault, and abuse me. Regardless of who I am or the decisions I made, I didn't deserve or ask for this. No one deserves or asks for abuse.

I will spend the rest of my life fighting for myself and fighting for those of you who see yourselves in my story.

It will never be your fault.

FIVE

The Aftermath

The aftermath of the last night with my ex-boyfriend was chaos mixed with healing and torture. I would forever doubt if the fallout was worth it. To this day, what keeps me grounded in knowing that I made the right decision to run and seek justice and healing are two very important reminders: (1) The lack of emotion and regard in his eyes as he attacked and hurt me, and (2) the women who never made it out of their situations and can't tell their stories. If for nothing else, I did this for those who cannot.

As I was taken via ambulance to the local emergency room, I peered out the back window and saw my friends staring after the ambulance with shock and fear, and my current boyfriend storming toward my ex-boyfriend, who had emerged from his house, which was now surrounded by crime scene investigators. It was the first and only time I ever saw my ex-boyfriend's face exhibit panic and fear. The ambulance turned the corner toward the hospital before I could see my current boyfriend being detained and the tears of my friends as they were being informed that they could meet me at the hospital.

Almost immediately after arriving at one of our local hospital emergency rooms, I was placed on a bed in a stark white, isolated room and joined by my university's rape-and-trauma advocate. She was calm, kind, and compassionate. She didn't look at me with pity but with strength and partnership. I felt immediately connected to her, as if she were an extension of me. She explained that if I consented, I would be questioned by police personnel and undergo medical assessments while at the hospital. She also told me that the questions and assessments would be the first step in an investigation into not only what occurred that night with my ex-boyfriend but my entire relationship with him. She said that while the city police would conduct the official investigation, the university would also conduct their own investigation on my behalf. She committed to staying with me during the entire process and said I could wait to move forward with the questioning and medical assessments until my friends and boyfriend arrived as a source of comfort. When I agreed to the questions and assessments, I didn't understand the weight of what would follow. It didn't register that I was agreeing to move forward with criminal investigations of my ex-boyfriend. It would be weeks before the gravity of the situation hit me.

When my friends arrived, my girlfriend who had tried to keep me from visiting my ex volunteered to join me in the room as solace. As you're reading this, I'm sure you're probably wondering how my current boyfriend could stand being part of that situation. He was and always will be a man who loved me to the depths of his soul. He endured a lot of pain because of me, and this night was one of the worst nights of his life. He became a rock and a confidante throughout all of this, and while our relationship would last on and off for years, ultimately I determined that staying together would prevent him from finding true happiness, and I couldn't let that happen.

When the university rape-and-trauma advocate left the room to let the police and medical personnel know I had agreed to the questioning and the medical procedures, my body started convulsing uncontrollably. As a premedical student and an avid fan of the medical drama *ER*, I realized my body was going into post-traumatic shock. When the university advocate returned to my convulsing body, I breathlessly told her I thought I was going into shock. Weeks later, she would tell me that she was floored by how keenly aware I was of my body. That awareness would be crucial throughout my road to recovery.

She immediately called in the rape-and-trauma nurse, and the two of them covered me in heated blankets until the convulsions subsided several minutes later. As my body calmed down, my emotions took over, and I started crying. The tears cascaded silently down my cheeks, and my girlfriend clutched my hand and didn't let go for the rest of the night. My energy was expended, and it felt like the tears were my heart's reaction to the trauma.

That night, I spent hours in the hospital talking to detectives about what had happened and endured an uncomfortable and painful sexual-assault forensic exam, or "rape kit." My blood was drawn to test for sexually transmitted diseases, and I was given several medications to prevent disease and other infections. By the time my friends and boyfriend took me home, I was so physically and emotionally drained and sick that I puked up everything in a cascade of rainbow colors.

Reality set in the next morning. The entire disaster started on Friday night and ended early Saturday morning. Unlike a typical college student, I was a college cheerleader. My Saturdays were filled with sporting events, cheerleading competitions, or events where the college cheerleaders represented the university. My university's rape-and-trauma advocate would prove to be a godsend for months to come. She learned everything about my classes and activities so she could contact my professors and cheerleading coaches to let them know I had endured a trauma that would deeply affect me. She helped me navigate every part of my university responsibilities.

The one responsibility she couldn't navigate with me was my responsibility to my parents. Since I was legally an adult, my parents did not have to be notified by the police or hospital; that was entirely my decision. I considered the easy option of not telling them and just letting life unfold as it may. Knowing I was a terrible liar and that my mother, especially, would notice something was different, I opted for the difficult yet right decision to call them Saturday morning. I gave them the Reader's Digest version and explained that the investigation would be ongoing, especially if I decided to prosecute. My mother's response was simple and quick: she would come pick me up that morning and I would stay at least the weekend with my family.

The car ride was awkward at best. As a naturally lively and boisterous family, the forty-five-minute car ride home was one of the longest bouts of silence I've ever endured with my mother. While my mother is not the touchy-feely type, she is always one to hug and kiss me when she sees me. Now, she didn't touch me or look at me. I would learn weeks later that she felt she had failed me as a mother. She didn't know how to help me, and she didn't recognize the look in my eyes. She said I looked hollow and fragile, not like the energized and loving woman she had raised.

When my mom and I arrived at my parents' house, it was clear she and my dad were tense and had been in the middle of a disagreement before she left to pick me up. Later that evening, the disagreement would continue. They had conflicting responses to my situation. Since both have a background in counseling, most people assume they would have had a logical response to the situation and known how to handle this trauma, but when your child is hurting and you can't help her, there's nothing logical about your response. My mother empathized and tried to figure out how to cope. My father was angry at me, at my ex-boyfriend, and at the entire situation and couldn't rationalize what it meant. Years later, they would be my greatest source of strength in dealing with the continued aftermath of this trauma, but at that moment, they were vulnerable and honest parents who couldn't save their daughter from a nightmarish situation.

Shortly after arriving home, I wandered the house aimlessly, not sure where to go or what to do. Lou was in college, but Julius and Faythe were still young enough to live at home. They wouldn't find out the reason I came home until almost a decade later. All they knew was I wasn't feeling well and I needed to be home for the weekend.

I didn't have a bedroom anymore, so I camped out in my parents' bedroom. Everyone handles trauma differently. For me, I felt such a lack of control that my response during the early stages of trauma was to organize the things within my control. The only thing I remember actively doing when I was home was organizing my mother's closet. My mother is a fashionista, meaning she has at least a million pairs of shoes and twice as many outfits. Her closet was a war zone at best. The door constantly stood open because the brightly colored dresses and variety of heels poured out of the doorway searching for a place to live.

Because I was unusually quiet, my mother came looking for me and found me sitting in her closet surrounded by high heels. She propped herself up on her bed and busied herself with whatever it was she needed to keep her mind focused. Years later, I would learn I did a horrible job of organizing her closet. In my blinded and numb state, I did nothing more than move shoes around so she couldn't find them. What was important to my mother at that moment was that I was able to bring control to at least one situation. She knew it was going to be an uphill battle for me, and if haphazardly organizing her closet brought me peace, then she would leave me to that peace.

I was only home for the weekend. The anxiety of missing out on school was overwhelming, and my parents knew I needed to try to return to at least one thing in my life that was still normal.

My life changed drastically when I returned to Wake. While I was gone for barely forty-eight hours, it felt like an entire lifetime had passed since that traumatic night. By the time I was back in my classes on Monday, my rape-and-trauma advocate had met with each of my professors and both of my cheerleading coaches to fill them in with need-to-know information on what to expect with a student who had endured trauma. I had private meetings with my professors, who offered extensions on upcoming exams and papers. In the haze of not quite realizing that my life had completely altered, I declined the extensions. It was the second semester of my junior year, and I was a communication major with premedical concentration. The last thing I wanted to do was add on more time to my already-slammed schedule.

Ironically, that semester would be the only semester that my grades were good enough to make the President's list—an honor for which the criteria was a 3.0 GPA (B average) or higher. At a university like Wake Forest, or as we liked to call it, "Work Forest," a 3.0 GPA was revered and admired. The university earned its nickname by being difficult at best. While it appeared most universities started their students on a grace system with an A average, our ongoing, not-so-funny joke at Wake was that it seemed like students started at a C average and had to work their way up.

The trauma released a temporary "genius brain" mentality. My mind was so warped and confused that the only thing I could control was my focus on my schoolwork. Sadly, that genius-brain mentality lasted only one semester, and my brain returned to the chaotic mess that it had been by the first semester of my senior year.

In addition to a grueling class schedule, we were also in the middle of basketball season at an Atlantic Coast Conference (ACC) university. The ACC was known for its exceptional basketball programs, and we were at the height of our basketball prowess. It was during the days of now-NBA-powerhouse Chris Paul, better known as CP3. Wake dominated the basketball scene, which meant lots of games! We would easily cheer three to four games in a given week.

During that time, I was cheering for both women's and men's basketball. One of my coaches graciously asked if I wanted to sit out that week or at least the first game. Since the first game happened to be a women's game, with typically lower attendance, I declined his offer. Talk about a poor choice! I didn't understand that trauma manifests itself in ways that don't always have to do directly with the traumatic situation. As soon as we left the locker room and walked toward the basketball court, all I could see were the crowds and lights. I immediately succumbed to sheer panic. My body reacted to something I couldn't understand, something I still don't understand. I raced back into the locker room, where I remained until halftime with my head between my knees, in and out of a panic attack.

That first game back, in my new normal, was the only one where I had a panic attack. My keen sense of body awareness paid off, as I could sense when I needed to slow down before heading into the crowds of people at the basketball games. I became aware of this coping technique well ahead of counseling and trauma therapy, which would equip me with valuable tools and resources to help me begin to live a life that wasn't filled with panic attacks and numbness.

Reflecting on the first week following my trauma puts me back in the shoes of a twenty-year-old college student who was devastated, numb, and afraid of the next steps. It also allows me to move forward as a midthirties successful professional who can see where she came from and the journey it took to get to this point of realization and healing. Everyone needs support when it comes to healing. I am grateful that I was surrounded by a supportive family, loving friends, and an extensive amount of counseling and therapy. As I've mentioned before, my faith is important to me, and I am a firm believer in God providing the resources for healing and not just blindly following religion and spirituality.

Resources look different to everyone. I encourage you not to allow someone else to dictate the way you seek help. I had some people in my life who I thought were friends but ended up causing more harm than good. One such friend, who would apologize to me years later but never fully return to my life as a trusted friend, thought "tough love" was the answer. He berated me and put me down for allowing myself to get into this situation. One of my true girlfriends who joined me at the hospital the night of the trauma stuck up for me and helped me end that friendship. He wasn't the right person to have at my side during that season of my life, but she was the person who would always have my back.

It would take over a decade for me to weed out the unhealthy relationships that didn't support my healing. I think we all struggle with that from time to time, and to be honest, it is still a work in progress. But my journey to healing and your journey to healing are 100 percent worth the time, energy, and difficulty it takes to align the right resources and right people in our lives.

SIX

You Can't Do This Life Alone

As the daughter of two counselors who also had their own home-based counseling business, I grew up eavesdropping on a lot of private conversations. I was fascinated by human behavior and even more fascinated by my parents' keen ability to openly listen and connect with even the most unique individuals.

My first real memory of a counseling session comes from back in the early- to mid-nineties. I was about ten years old, and we were living in Tuscaloosa, Alabama (a story for a later chapter). My parents were counselors for the church we attended and used our home as a safe place for church members.

My parents were well known in our church, primarily for their innate people skills, but also because we were the only black family in the church. They were in their midthirties when we lived in Alabama, young enough that young people related to them but old enough to have knowledge and wisdom.

My two youngest siblings were born during the five years that we lived there. My parents juggled four children ten years old and younger, jobs in the education industry, and their own thriving counseling business. I am now the exact same age they were then, and I can barely juggle myself, my career, and my dog and cat, both of which I only have part-time. My parents are beyond impressive to me now, and they were impressive to our church members back then.

One such person who was impressed with them was a seventeen-year-old man whom I will call Prince Charming. Prince Charming was my first true love. I was only eight years old, so I wasn't quite into the boy scene yet, but Prince Charming truly lived up to his name. We basically lived at this church, as did Prince Charming and his family. The church doubled as an accredited Christian school for infants through twelfth grade.

We had a lot of school/church events, from sporting events to musicals to fall festivals, especially around October as an alternative to traditional Halloween activities. Would you believe that I have never been trick-or-treating? Halloween was not something my parents supported. The older I became, the more my parents relaxed on some of their rules, but I still didn't want to trick-or-treat. There was something disturbing to super-introverted, shy me about knocking on a stranger's door and asking them to give me candy.

However, I absolutely loved the church's fall festivals, which were basically trick-or-treating in the church gym. My costume of choice from eight to ten years old was Belle from Beauty and the Beast. Prince Charming loved my Belle costume, and that was one of the reasons I loved him. The first time we met was my first year as Belle. He was working at the fall festival alongside the other teenagers. When I walked in, he came over to me and said, "I'm sorry; are you Miss America?" I was smitten!

My parents were chatting with all the other families, trying to control a very active six-year-old Lou and dropping off Julius in the nursery. Faythe would happily join the festivities the next year. Since they knew everyone there, including Prince Charming, they happily let him be my "date" for the night. He doted on me, held my hand, and introduced me as Miss America to everyone. I was petite, so sometimes he would pick me up and twirl me around. At eight years old, I remember thinking I could spend the rest of my life with Prince Charming.

I had no way of knowing the struggles Prince Charming was going through in his life. To this day, I purposely haven't asked my parents about his counseling sessions. When he came over to the house, it was usually late at night, and he always looked weathered and much older than a teenage boy. I noticed every time my dad greeted him at church, he always added an extra hug or a tight hand-hold. The strong feelings my parents had for Prince Charming drew me to him even more. I knew there was something beautiful and special about him, and I was so grateful to be part of his life.

Our last year in Alabama would be my last year spending time with Prince Charming. Late one evening when I was ten years old, we received a phone call that Prince Charming had been involved in a fatal motorcycle accident. His funeral was one of two gone-too-soon funerals we attended that year. A beloved sixteen-year-old girl at our church would also pass away in a car accident.

I remember feeling empty when I heard the news. I may have been a child, but I understood loss. Prince Charming had a gift he was sharing with the world. Though he had lots of demons that he was fighting, as we all do, he had something beautiful to offer life.

We left Alabama shortly after his passing and moved to North Carolina, where my parents continued their counseling ministry in our next home church. During that time, my father was a professor of counseling and expanding his counseling-specific consulting business. He received an offer not only to serve as a professor with a new university but also to work with a larger consulting group that could expand his influence.

Since I grew up with counselors as parents, you might think I was a well-adjusted kid. That couldn't be further from the truth. Having counselors as parents just means I am hyper-aware of what's going on in people's lives. I can spot disorders a mile away. There have been many times in my adult life when I've had to hold my tongue because the person I was interacting with was clearly exhibiting bipolar disorder attributes, and I felt like maybe it wasn't the time for me to share that tidbit of information.

My first personal experience with counseling was when I was about fourteen years old. I was having an emotionally rough day. Throughout my childhood, I exhibited tendencies toward anxiety, and the older I became, the more depression became part of my life. I cannot remember any triggers that led to the emotions of that day, but I know I was feeling unhinged and despondent. I "casually" mentioned to a good friend that things would be better if I just ended my life. Suicide is never anything to joke about, and though I was not entirely serious when I shared that with my friend, I was considering what it would be like to end things and not feel depressed anymore. She rightfully contacted our school counselor, who immediately contacted my parents. I didn't know they had been contacted until I came home after school, and my dad asked me to go for a drive with him. He talked with me about how I was feeling and shared that my friend was concerned that I might be suicidal. After assuring him I was fine—and by that point I actually was fine—he recommended I meet with the school counselor so she could better assess my feelings.

I was so angry with my friend! I thought she had betrayed me. When we returned home, I immediately called her and told her I didn't want to be friends anymore. It would be a few months before I apologized and thanked her for taking the right step to keep me safe.

The next day at school I had an appointment with one of our school guidance counselors. At best, this guidance counselor was incompetent. I was resistant to counseling from the beginning, so I was silent during our meeting. The guidance counselor not only glossed over the fact that I was asked to meet with her because I was suicidal, she had the audacity to make fun of me during the appointment. She laughed when we were discussing my potential depression and anxiety and mocked me when I raised an eyebrow in disbelief while she was laughing. She even scoffed at my "issues," letting me know she thought this was ridiculous. Returning for another appointment was not an option as far as I was concerned, and when I shared with my parents how unsuccessful the counseling visit was, they agreed.

I don't know if my parents ever had a conversation with the school or the counselor about her lack of ability, but I do know a few years later she was thankfully no longer in that role. I hate to go so far as saying she was unqualified; I think she was uninformed. In the nineties and early 2000s, mental health was rarely discussed and was surrounded by a negative stigma. To think about teenagers having any type of problems was unheard of.

While that was my first foray into counseling, it wouldn't be my last. I returned to counseling at the beginning of my junior year at Wake Forest, right when my ex-boyfriend reached out to me. My unnatural connection to him worried my friends who knew we were back in contact, and they encouraged me to seek advice from our university counselors. That counselor would prove to be a godsend, especially after the traumatic night that landed me in the hospital.

You might be surprised to know that during my counseling sessions, I was realizing my ex had an unhealthy hold on me and I needed to leave him. I was getting closer and closer to ending things the night he attacked me. The fact that I was already seeking help for an unhealthy relationship and mind-set saved my life. I don't know what would have happened to me if I had remained there that night, but I know I wouldn't be the person I am today—or even alive.

Following the traumatic night, an emergency appointment was scheduled with my counselor. I sat in that counseling session in complete, disconnected silence. It was the first of many sessions that I attended either completely disconnected or completely drunk. While drinking was not a normal occurrence for me, it became my go-to coping mechanism during the early aftermath of the trauma.

Within the first two weeks of my counseling sessions, I was put on suicide watch, and all of my knives, scissors, and other sharp objects were removed from my room. I started to self-harm to enhance the impact of the alcohol. I couldn't feel anything. I couldn't hear anything. I could barely breathe. It felt like I was living outside of my body, watching the train wreck of my life take place.

Self-harm helped me feel. I would slice the top of my thighs because it was impossible for anyone to see that part of my body unless I was naked, and then only if they were looking really closely. The pain mixed with relief I felt was temporary, but at least I felt something.

Counseling served as a haven away from the storm that was an uncontrollable barrage of emotions and feelings in my life. I originally saw my counselor monthly and then transitioned to one or two times per week. My counselor was my emergency speed dial and saved me from the demons that were taking over my life.

Every single person has a different story, and I can't tell you how to seek healing for your story. What I will tell you is we were not meant to live alone with trauma, depression, anxiety, or sorrow. I firmly believe in counseling. The stigma exists because we trick ourselves into believing that we were meant to handle everything on our own. Asking for help is seen as a weakness. I challenge that mind-set and consider asking for help a strength. The most successful people I know have an around-the-clock counselor because life is hard and it hurts.

Oftentimes I hear, "Well, good for you for having all of those resources around you, but counseling costs money that I do not have." You are absolutely right, but there are also nonprofit counseling services that cost little to no money or offer services using an income-based sliding scale. There are also free online support groups. When I graduated from Wake Forest, I spent five months in a job without benefits that paid me barely enough to cover my rent. I had no resources or money for any type of services, much less counseling. Online support groups were my saving grace. I could talk to others who understood how I was feeling and could walk me through what to expect next. Not every story is the same, but we all deserve the opportunity to feel valued and supported.

Never allow the stigma of what society tells you to stop you from seeking the help you need.

SEVEN

The Zone of Hot Mess

When I was told by my university counselor that I had post-traumatic stress disorder, I received the news in silence. I didn't understand what he was telling me. And I certainly didn't want to have a disorder label attached to my name.

For about four weeks following the last night with my ex, I exhibited erratic, dangerous behavior. When my counselor explained to me that the feelings and behaviors I was experiencing were a reaction to the trauma I had been through, I shut off even more. I didn't want to be part of the "PTSD club." The stigma surrounding any type of disorder, much less PTSD, meant I had a "scarlet letter" attached to me that everyone could see. I was a twenty-year-old college student, not an older man who had experienced war or other traumatic events. According to television and movies, I did not fit the profile for a PTSD sufferer.

Regardless of what I thought PTSD should or should not look like, I did fit the bill. My erratic behavior was only the beginning of a long, terrifying journey into what I call "the Zone of Hot Mess." My emotions and hormones were out of control at best. One moment I was stoic, another manic, another enraged, and then I was the life of the party. In my head, I was the only person in my universe. It wasn't that I didn't *care* how people were impacted by my actions, it's that I didn't *see* how people were impacted by my actions. I was in a cone of hysteria where I was barely hanging on to my own sanity. I lacked the ability to worry about other people when I couldn't even worry about myself.

Shortly after my diagnosis, I was introduced to an antidepressant-antianxiety pill. The first prescribed dosage was just potent enough to make me angry and even more suicidal. After a quick prescription upgrade, the higher dosage made me feel numb and hollow. I preferred neither feeling, but I also didn't have a death wish, so I continued with the higher dosage. I give the medication credit. My emotions and hormones were so unstable that I am positive I wouldn't have made it past my twentieth year without them.

Although the medication brought me to a place of emotional steadiness, the numbness that accompanied the steadiness was preventing me from experiencing actual feelings. I knew I wasn't completely stable off the medication, but I also knew I couldn't keep living in a trance, not owning my actions and my feelings. That, coupled with the stigma of how others, even my family, felt about me taking medication, was enough for me to try to cope on my own. During my mid- to late twenties, I worked with my physician and counselors to steadily wean myself off the medication.

After stopping the medication, I spent my late twenties and early thirties trying to live a "normal" life. I was fine for the most part, with occasional random bouts of intense anxiety and hysteria, until the random bouts escalated. After six to seven years without medication, I realized that therapy, coping tools, and prayer would only help so much, and that I am someone who needs more assistance and balance. I know God provides each of us with the resources we need to live out His plan in our lives. My resource just happens to include a beautiful little pill that keeps me from acting like the girl from *The Exorcist* when I am having an off day.

Everyone has opinions about the use of medication. This is a personal decision, and no one can tell you whether a medication is right for you. This must come from you and your conversation with your own medical professional. I am open and honest enough to admit that I still take an antianxiety medication. This medication has no negative side effects, and it does take the edge off the persistent anxiety I experience that is escalated by my PTSD.

PTSD is a disorder that takes hold of every part of who you are and destroys it, leaving you an empty shell, barely able to understand who you are or who you are supposed to be. There are many lingering side effects from PTSD: flashback nightmares, panic attacks, anxiety disorder, depression, suicidal thoughts, self-harm, memory loss—the list goes on. Even after medication was introduced, some of those side effects didn't subside for years. Some of them are still present.

Around the time of my diagnosis, when I was prescribed medication for the first time and the numbness took over, I moved beyond just slicing the top of my thighs. I was now digging holes into my hands with my own fingernails until they bled. I was taking drunken joyrides, hoping to run into someone or something to end it all. I was having sex with any guy who flirted with me because it made me feel like a "normal" college student. I was also promptly freaking out during my sexual encounters because I would have immediate flashbacks to my ex-boyfriend. My life was, by all definitions, a hot mess.

My girlfriends treated me like glass and tried to arrange for one person to have eyes on me every day. I was running them ragged and running myself into the ground. I realized early on that my behavior was destructive, but I just didn't care. Every single night, I was either wide awake with panic and the fear that my ex would come back and kill me, or I was sleeping, immersed in horrible nightmares, reliving that last night we were together. I desperately wanted an escape from the demons plaguing my mind, my body, and my heart.

I am completely aware that had I not been at a small, private university where not only was my counselor on campus but my friends also had almost immediate access to him, I would be in a very different place in my life. I learned later that when we left the hospital, my university's rape-and-trauma advocate connected with my friends to give them information about how to seek counseling if they desired it. When I first started counseling prior to the hospital visit, I had shared with my friends who my counselor was, which allowed them to reach out to him to share any concerns. I am forever grateful for the connection my friends had to my counselor, even though, at the time, I didn't realize they were saving my life.

While the counseling helped ground me, it did little to help me deal with my chaotic and destructive thinking. By the time I graduated from Wake Forest, I was so consumed with myself and my hot-mess journey that I had no plans following graduation. As a communication major with a premedical concentration, you would think medical school or a paid internship at a television studio would have been in the works for me. But the only concrete plan I had was to continue my side job of coaching cheerleading at the local cheerleading gym, which paid just enough to cover my portion of the rent for a house I shared with two other women.

Upon graduation, I was introduced to the idea of joining the military, specifically the Army. While I have an uncle who is now a retired lieutenant in the Navy and a scattering of cousins enlisted in the Army, my military knowledge was limited. Nonetheless, what intrigued me was that the Army would pay for me to go to medical school if I made a twelve-year commitment to serving, which included the years I would be in medical school. Seeing a semblance of hope, structure, and direction that I desperately needed, I jumped at the opportunity to attend an introduction to the Army orientation course.

By August 2007, three months following my graduation from Wake Forest, I was on my way to Fort Bragg, North Carolina. My parents' house was about one hour closer to Fort Bragg than my current house, so I went there the night before I was supposed to leave so that I would have a shorter drive the next morning.

The next morning, as my dad was closing the garage door, I began driving down the road in front of their house. The garage door was halfway closed when the ball joint in the driver's side tire and wheelbase popped out of my car. My car steered itself into a ditch and flipped over onto its roof. Once I realized I was in a ditch and upside down, panic threatened to set in. I knew if I panicked I would be stuck, so I wrested myself right side up in time to see a very tall, very dark-skinned man driving by my car. He appeared out of nowhere, and I had no time to register any other distinguishing features. He stopped, climbed into the ditch, helped me pry open the car door, assisted me out of the car and the ditch, and placed me on the side of the road. Amid tears of relief, I pointed out my parents' house, and he simultaneously called 9-1-1 and ran to talk to my father. My dad rushed over to me, and I assumed the stranger would be behind him, but he and his car had already disappeared as if they were never there. We never saw that man again. The neighborhood my parents lived in at the time was a neighborhood where everyone knew everyone. When we described this man to others in the neighborhood, nobody could identify him. Some said it was clearly a blessed coincidence. I firmly believe he was a guardian angel.

The volunteer firefighters were the first to arrive on the scene, and after seeing the car wreck, they immediately stabilized me on a stretcher until the ambulance arrived to take me to the hospital. When the firefighters and EMS crew were questioning me, they asked several times if I was sure I had been driving. I learned later that not only was my car completely totaled, but the driver's side was smashed in through the dashboard. I walked away with a surface laceration across my knee that required twenty stitches and an eye-opening perspective on the reality of not taking life for granted.

This new perspective and gratitude would be short-lived, as I realized I was carless, and the one opportunity that could have aligned me with a career direction had been quashed in the car accident.

There wouldn't be another Army orientation for another year, but to be honest, not going to Fort Bragg was a blessing in disguise. I no longer had a passion for practicing medicine, but I still had no idea what I wanted to do. The only thing I knew was I was steadily losing my sanity from my PTSD, I had no method of transportation to get me to the job that could help me pay my rent, and I had no career direction. The circumstances of my life were exacerbating all the side effects of my PTSD, and I was moving into a very dark place.

During my senior year, my counselor told me that when I graduated, the university's counseling services would no longer be available. He knew I needed more than counseling, and instead of recommending another counselor, he referred me to a trauma therapist. While the referral was a great idea, as you can imagine, I had few to no resources available to pay for the desperately needed trauma therapy. From the end of May 2007 to October 2007 I was without counseling services during a time when I needed it most. That may seem like just a few months to some, but for someone struggling with PTSD, it felt like a lifetime. I was hobbling around with a lacerated knee; I was carless, unable to work, and directionless.

Yes, I understand life could have been much worse, but as far as I was concerned, all I could see was unending misery. I felt like I was a disgrace to myself and to my family because I just couldn't figure my life out. Luckily, I was still under my mother's insurance, so I could continue to take my antianxiety-antidepressant medication, but the small amount of money I needed for the copay for that medication was quickly running out.

I needed some type of employment fast. I ended up applying for and getting a job as a photographer for a photography studio chain. I am not a photographer. I can't even take pictures on my phone without having to retake them at least twice. Forget taking selfies—it's more like taking a hundred selfies, and the first one ends up being the best of the worst. During the interview for the position, I embellished my leadership skills, and my Wake Forest background was impressive enough for them to ignore my inability to take an actual photograph. The job was sufficient to get me on my feet. I could cover my rent and also connect with the trauma therapist my counselor had referred me to.

The therapy, even under my mother's insurance, was eighty dollars a session. That's a lot of money to pay to have someone tell you you're not OK! I arrived at my first appointment thinking, *One and done, then I'm fixed!* It turned out to be more like one of many and never done.

My trauma therapist had the calm, soothing nature that you see in all the movies. When I walked into her office, I was surprised there wasn't a couch available for me to lie down on and share my feelings.

She had received my background information from my university counselor, but she wanted to hear my reasons for coming to see her from me. We spent the first session reliving my relationship with my ex-boyfriend. At the conclusion of the session, she asked if I had heard of EMDR (eye movement desensitization and reprocessing) therapy. It sounded like she was going to attach electrodes to me, so I skeptically said no, I wasn't certain it was for me. I was also secretly concerned that EMDR would cost an additional eighty dollars, and I would end up destitute from therapy. When she explained it was not going to cost extra and that all I had to do was try it once, I reluctantly agreed.

Eye movement desensitization and reprocessing therapy is an eight-phase treatment in which patients relive their traumatic experiences while a therapist diverts their attention by directing their eye movements. The therapist may move his or her hand across the patient's field of vision or, as in my case, provide small, battery-operated, vibrating nodules that are held in each hand. As they vibrated, I closed my eyes so that my eyes could track the vibrations. Having your attention diverted allows you to experience the traumatic memories without having a strong psychological response, eventually lessening the impact of these memories.

EMDR turned out to be the therapy I needed to provide long-term coping for a lifelong disorder.

Prior to my first EMDR appointment, my trauma therapist prepared me for the side effects of the therapy. The sessions themselves would require me to return to the trauma, knowing that my brain would steadily process through the trauma to provide empowerment and strength by the end of the eight sessions. Each session would last about ninety minutes, but the first was two hours long to ensure I had enough cushion time before and after to prepare and process. She explained that I should make sure I didn't have to go to work or make any long trips after each appointment. Extreme exhaustion followed each session because of the work the brain goes through to reprocess the events, and at the conclusion of each, I would pass out for at least two hours.

The first session was simultaneously terrifying and comforting. As my brain took me back to the trauma, I felt myself physically reacting and tears coursing down my face, but when I felt like the pain was too much, my therapist would push me to find the safest place in my mind. That safe place was St. Augustine Beach with my parents when I was a small child. They would take us there during the summer when we lived in Florida, and I remember feeling safe, secure, and happy during those times. That safe place has not changed. When I feel anxiety building in my life now, I go back in my mind to the beach, any beach. As long as I can visualize the cool sand, crisp open air, and soothing sound of waves, I feel safe.

Over the eight sessions (one each month), I steadily regained sanity. I was able to cope with any triggers, such as a car that looked like my ex-boyfriend's, or someone raising their voice at or near me. I was starting to live my life and focus on my future. My brain was reprocessing, so it was no longer consumed with the trauma but was starting to revert to understanding other aspects of life. I found myself having direction again.

In February 2008, I found another job that didn't require me to take pictures of screaming children and not-so-cooperative parents. I started a position back in the healthcare industry as an executive assistant for a contract physical rehabilitation company. The CEO of the company owned a fitness gym and a mixed-martial-arts fighting gym, and he needed someone to run the administrative and operational side of his company.

The job helped bring me back to a place where I felt driven and passionate about my life again. I felt like I had direction and purpose, and coupled with the trauma therapy, I was able to think through what made sense for me to pursue in my life. The CEO of the company is still someone I consider a trusted advisor, mentor, and friend. He didn't know the trauma I was experiencing, but he saw something beautiful and bright in me that he nurtured. That job helped bring me to a place where the Zone of Hot Mess dissipated and was replaced by the Journey toward Healing.

Like many, if not all, disorders, post-traumatic stress disorder (PTSD) has its own stigmas and stereotypes. When I tell someone I have PTSD, the first question I hear is, "Were you in the military?" When my respectful but immediate answer is no, it is almost always followed by a look of confusion, then silence. The follow-up question, "What happened?" rarely comes next. I can see it in their eyes, but often they refrain from asking.

Now, over ten years after being diagnosed and after about five years of sharing my story, I don't allow the silence to obscure my story. While I don't share the details unless someone asks for them, I do share the reality that my PTSD didn't just happen—it was from years of sexual assault, rape, and abuse. I am also quick to share that it never goes away and it's not easy, but I wouldn't be who I am if I didn't make a point to survive and thrive from this experience.

I will never say that I am grateful for the pain and trauma my ex-boyfriend put me through. I will always say I am a strong, resilient, and accomplished woman. The trauma I went through didn't and doesn't own me. I made a choice to be honest about not being OK. I made a choice to seek help, and I made a choice to share my story.

Know and believe that you too can make choices. You have choices and a chance to be more than the pain you feel every day. What choice do you need to make to move forward? Is it the choice to contact a counselor, an online support group, or a medical professional? Is it the choice to let go of that unhealthy person or obsession? Whatever it is, I cannot tell you how to take the first step. That is and will always be a personal decision and a personal conviction. What I can say is that taking that first step can save your life. If you are living in the shadows of your own demons and pain, you aren't living the life you were meant to live.

Make the choice to own your next step.

EIGHT

Unexpected Lessons

My mom has been my role model since I was born. She is by no means perfect, but she is the epitome of a woman who understands that the difficulty of life's circumstances may not always get you where you want to be, but it sure will teach you how to drive toward something and somewhere even better.

My mother's family emigrated from Jamaica to America in the 1960s and '70s. My grandmother was the first to arrive, with the goal of gaining better opportunities for herself and her family. Her oldest son, my uncle, followed shortly after and enlisted in the Navy upon his arrival in America. My grandfather spent several years raising my mom and her five siblings until opportunities opened up for them to move to America. By 1977, they were all reunited and focused on gaining better opportunities in a new country.

Most people underestimate the culture shock of immigrating to a new country, especially a country that seems like it's just a hop, skip, and jump away from America. There are entirely different customs, constructs, and rules for every country. When I talked to my mom about her first experiences in America, she said they were less than pleasant. She had a thick, non-American accent and light-colored, not-quite-brown skin; was incredibly shy and insecure; and didn't understand the expectations of American culture.

When she immigrated at seventeen years old, she had already completed high school. Because the American school system saw her as too young to go to college, they required that she enroll and complete her senior year in high school. She didn't feel as if she fit in, and she didn't understand why the kids didn't accept her just because she was different. In Jamaican culture, you're not really categorized as black, white, or mixed; you're just Jamaican, and there is an unspoken camaraderie associated with that.

Jamaicans maintain that mentality even outside of Jamaica. With my travels, I am immersed in a lot of different cultures. One of my favorite experiences is showing up at a hotel to check in and hearing the distinctive Jamaican-islander lilt from a fellow traveler or hotel staff member. People not exposed to the Caribbean culture will easily confuse a Haitian lilt with a Bahamian lilt with a Jamaican lilt, but those of us who grew up with the accent can subtly distinguish one from the other.

During these cultural experiences, my first question is always, "Where are you originally from?" Typically, I get a smile and an immediate "Jamaica." The next question is the icing on the cake for any Jamaican meeting another Jamaican: "What part of Jamaica?" I always share that my mother grew up in the mountains of Jamaica, in Mandeville, and then a we-are-just-like-family strangers' reunion ensues. (And, yes, there are mountains in Jamaica. I am as shocked as you are, but my mother swears they exist!)

It's a comforting thing to feel connected to someone because you share a cultural background. That connection didn't exist for my mother during her brief American high school experience. The cultural experience was foreign enough, but the schooling was vastly different. The concept of standardized testing was quite different, especially the ever-revered Scholastic Aptitude Test, or as most of us know it, the SAT. For an American, the analogies, math equations, and other torture devices on the SAT seem difficult but doable. For someone not familiar with common American sayings and lacking years of American schooling, the SAT is like a torture device for the brain and soul. It made no sense to my mother, and quite honestly, the SAT made no sense to me when I took it more than twenty years later.

My mother worked hard to learn the educational system. According to her siblings, as the middle of seven children, she always had a fierce determination to do whatever she set her mind to do. Determination does not always mean an easy path, though. While she didn't excel in her first and only year of American schooling, she did successfully complete her senior year and was accepted into the University of Florida, where she would earn several degrees, and eventually, in her midfifties (she would never forgive me for revealing her age), she would trade in her Mrs. for Dr. and become one of three Dr. Tobiases in our family. Oh, and let's not forget: all of this while raising a family of four children and a husband—let's be honest, a husband or spouse comes with an entirely different set of responsibilities.

My mother's experiences influenced the lessons she imparted. She and my father both taught us to always strive for our goals, regardless of other people's opinions. She also taught us to listen and keep our hearts and minds open to the people around us. Don't just blow someone off because they are different. Instead, embrace them because there is something they can teach you that you wouldn't learn without their unique perspective.

Most people play the comparison game with social media; I play the comparison game with people close to me, like my mother. Reflecting on my upbringing and my mother's life, I constantly find myself thinking, *What was my mom doing at my age?* especially when I'm exhausted or feeling beaten down or just plain unaccomplished. At thirty-four, while I'm juggling personal relationships and striving toward the next step in my career, my mother had recently welcomed baby number four, was conquering the world one philosophical thought at a time, and working as a high school counselor. Though I know my journey is different from hers, I find myself questioning whether I am on the right path. Am I making the right choices, choosing the right people, opening myself up to the right experiences?

When I share these concerns with my mother, as my best friend, she never hesitates to say, "Your path is different, and it should be. I don't want for you what God intended for me." She is my biggest supporter and my biggest deliverer of constructive feedback. She has always said that in order to achieve God's plan, you must be willing not only to put in the work but also to be uncomfortable when you can't see what God is trying to do in your life through that work. She has also instilled in me the understanding that greatness involves great risk, great reward, great failure, and great pioneering. You may find yourself on a path all your own, without the immediate guidance of someone who has navigated that path before you to shape the direction you should go. However, living in this day and in this country, there are countless men and women who have opened doors that we have a responsibility to walk through and create an even more pronounced path for those who will follow us.

Struggling through the emotional turmoil of PTSD is work in and of itself, especially when I feel like I am living the journey alone. Striving for something greater in my life, for the plan I know God has laid out, is terrifying. Most days . . . well, let's be honest—every single day, I struggle to see His plan. One of the pastors at my church recently asked me to join her podcast as a guest speaker to discuss women owning their leadership skills. She openly shared how impressed she was with my accomplishments, and the first questions she asked me were how I got to where I was and whether my career choice had always been my dream. I told her bluntly that I failed a lot before I could achieve the success I have now. I spent many seasons frustrated and angry because I had no idea what God was doing in my life, and it just felt like one big mess. Pioneering my current path came with a lot of focused work, failed attempts, and, just like my mother, fierce determination.

From my childhood through high school, I planned to become a pediatric surgeon. I followed a specific academic path that would lead me to becoming a certified nursing assistant (CNA) by the time I graduated high school. I spent most of my senior year in high school finishing my certification through clinical rotations in the local hospital and nursing homes and training under seasoned nurses and physicians. I assisted in surgeries, cared for the elderly, and held countless babies. I remember almost every single patient I cared for, and I learned on day one that it took more than academic studies to become a healthcare provider. Though I spent only a few years clinically caring for patients, this start to my healthcare career would shape the way I approached patients, healthcare workers, and dare I say life, moving forward.

I was a bit of a hard-ass when I started my clinical rotations, and gratefully, my nursing leader was focused on breaking my tough exterior. I was prideful because I quickly picked up on the medical terminology and excelled at the academic side of our nursing-assistant testing. When we were introduced to the people side of care, during my first week, our nursing leader assigned me to two of the most memorable patients of my career. In the nursing home, I was assigned to an elderly woman in the last stage of her life who was under around-the-clock care. During that same week, in my rotation at the hospital, I was assigned to the neonatal intensive care unit (NICU), where premature babies were cared for, and one of the babies under my care was born addicted to cocaine to a fourteen-year-old mother who rarely, if ever, visited her.

Both patients needed more than clinical care and book smarts. They needed love, affection, and compassionate care. My NICU patient gripped my heart and showed me the vulnerability and innocence of newborn life. Her bassinet was in the far corner of one of the NICU rooms, and her body was covered in dark, foil-like material to keep her cool and shielded from light. The cocaine coursing through her body at such a fragile age created an intolerable sensitivity to light, and she cried and sobbed in pain incessantly. Soothing her was my primary role. We had to be careful moving her, so I would stand over her bassinet cooing to her, lightly caressing her, and expressing my love to her for hours during the day. During my stay with her, she would have no visitors, and she seemed to soak up every touch and every kind word she received from me or other nursing team members.

While my heart ached for my newborn patient, my heart broke for my much older patient in the nursing home. During my first shift with this patient, I was sitting alone next to her bedside, as her family had just left to freshen up before returning that evening. Instead of calming and soothing this patient, I spent most of my time monitoring her breathing and incessantly fighting with her as she constantly tried to claw off her oxygen mask. At the end of life, people react differently, and some people become belligerent. She was part of the population of people who are belligerent. I felt as if I were fighting a battle for my life right alongside her. Every ten to fifteen minutes, she would lash out with sharp, bony hands and try violently to wrench her oxygen mask from her face.

Every ten to fifteen minutes, I questioned what made me qualified to handle any type of medical care, especially that of a woman whom I considered a raving lunatic at the end of her life. I ended my first shift of her care angry, disheartened, and convinced my nursing leader was playing a sick joke on me because she disliked me. When she asked me how my day went, I answered through gritted teeth that it was fine and stormed off. I couldn't fathom why she wasn't using my skills to help care for patients who weren't combative and why it even made sense for anyone to give this woman care, seeing she clearly didn't appreciate it.

The next day, when I showed up for my shift in the nursing home to care for my combative patient, I wasn't alone in her room. Her family was there, and they had been instructed to allow the medical professional (me) to take care of any combative situations, and to try to be patient and understanding. Reluctantly and with as negative an attitude as seventeen-year-old me could muster, I said I understood. I was not pleased about being back in this same assignment yet again. I had desperately hoped my nursing leader had seen the fault of her ways and reassigned me. Realizing that was not the case, I acquiesced to what I considered the worst part of my day. Before I walked into the room, my leader stopped me and advised me that this could be the last day this family would see their mother, and I should remember that the end of life is just as precious as the beginning.

When I walked into the room, the family turned toward me with tears in their eyes and apologies on their lips. Her daughter said something that I remember verbatim more than seventeen years later: "I am so sorry. This is not the mother we grew up with. I know that she has been volatile and that it's been hard to take care of her, but trust me when I say she used to be the kindest, sweetest woman, and she wouldn't hurt anyone." The admonishment of my nursing leader to remember how precious the end of life is resounded in my head, and I said words that, in my immaturity, I never expected to say. I told her, "It's OK. My job is to care for your mother in the best way I possibly can, and that's exactly what I'm going to do. I'm here for you and her."

That day, she was even more combative than the previous day, but I barely noticed. I spent the majority of my time thinking about how I could make sure this family felt that their mother was receiving the same gentleness and kindness that I gave to the NICU baby, and that I would give to every single one of my patients moving forward. When she violently grabbed for her oxygen mask, I gently removed her hand and said soothing words to her, using her first name and assuring her that we were all there for her.

When I ended my shift, her daughter asked if she could talk to me. With tears in her eyes, she simply said, "Thank you for showing my mother the same dignity and grace you would show to any patient during the last stage of her life." When I walked out of the room and my nursing leader asked me how my day was, I finally broke down, and through sobs, I told her it was the most important day of my life. Later that evening, my patient passed away, surrounded by her family. The next day, I mourned her loss with the rest of my classmates and restarted my healthcare career with a focus on compassion and love.

Each of our paths is different. We can drive ourselves crazy playing the comparison game, wondering why our lives can't be like a certain celebrity's, friend's, or even our own family members'. Or why our jobs can't be easier, or our families less dysfunctional. I would never have learned compassionate care and truly compassionate living had I not had the experiences I did during my first official week of my healthcare career. After that week, I encountered so many other patients who needed a friendly touch, a smile, or just someone to connect with.

Ultimately, I found that while the clinical side of healthcare was intriguing, it wasn't my passion. I loved helping to solve the problems that other people could not with the processes, workflows, and people that make up healthcare. Although I could do the clinical work, I didn't feel connected to it as much as I did to growing and developing the people who provide clinical care.

The same compassion I used in my clinical care is what I use in my work as a consultant. It's difficult as a leader of a company to say you don't have all the answers. It takes vulnerability and strength to call in someone who can help you rebuild and refocus on a path that will lead your company or hospital to success instead of failure. And it takes compassion for the person you call in to meet you where you are and say, "You know what? We will work through this together."

Instead of questioning your path, embrace your path. Open yourself up to whomever you may need to share your compassion with along the way. The lessons you are learning may help to carve someone else's path. They need you to own your journey, or they won't be able to own their journey. Don't be afraid to embrace the chaos of your life and learn the unexpected lessons that will help you survive and thrive through it all.

NINE

I Am and Always Will Be Enough

I have done all of you a great injustice. I deeply apologize for this, but the time has come for me to be honest with myself and all of you: I am a black woman. I know. I am shocked as well. The truth is, I have always been a black woman. Take some time to process that. I know—still shocked. I am also an intelligent woman, an accomplished woman, a traumatized woman, a woman who thinks she is gorgeous, and a woman who sometimes thinks her "wine belly" is scaring away all of her potential male suitors. But through it all, one of the many things that remains the same is I am a black woman.

The color of my skin, the articulation of my words, and the tone of my voice are constantly open for debate. I can't tell you how many times people of all races have said, "Wow! You don't talk black," or "You're so pretty for a black girl," or my all-time favorite, "You don't really count as being black." As you read this, I'm sure you're thinking, *Well, that must have been* way *back in the day.* No, my friend. Just a few weeks ago I was in a Lyft with a black, female driver, probably in her midfifties, at one of the many airports I visit during my work trips.

After I reserved the Lyft, the driver called me prior to picking me up to make sure I knew where to meet her. While my picture is on the Lyft app, when I hopped into the backseat, her first words were, "Well, you didn't seem like a sista on the phone. You're like my grandkids. They're not really all-the-way black either. They talk like you."

What in the world is "all-the-way black"? Is it like chicken when it's not all the way cooked? At nine in the morning, after having been up since four thirty that morning to begin yet another early-morning travel day, my mind told me to engage in a productive conversation on race, but my heart told me, "Girl, take a nap." So nap I did, but clearly the one-sided conversation is still buried deep in my mind.

Growing up Jamaican, categorizing someone's stereotypical actions, speech, or attributes based on the color of his or her skin isn't a priority. Jamaicans are Jamaicans, and we embrace that culture and are proud to share it with the world. While that is the mind-set I still have in my heart, I am intimately aware that in American culture, the deep chocolate color of my skin results in automatic categorization, stereotyping, and even visceral responses from people who can't believe I'm allowed out in public. I have walked by a nonblack (shall we say white?) woman in my business suit and high heels and watched her clutch her purse and nearly break her neck and back trying not to be touched by me. One time when I was in a more frustrated mood, I looked one of these "special" ladies directly in the eyes and said, "It doesn't rub off." And with the tone of my voice, I was adding, "You should be so lucky if it did."

While I now consider myself extremely proud and grateful to be a black woman in America, that pride took a lot of personal growth, bitter and angry conversations, and self-reflection on the message I wanted people to take away after meeting me. I would love to say I have grown to a point in my life where I don't care what people think of me, but that will never be the case. With age has come the wisdom to not allow people's opinions to be any of my business, but I will always care deep down inside if the person staring at me awkwardly or whispering and looking in my direction has a problem with me.

Race will always be an issue as long as people are uncomfortable with another person who doesn't look, think, or talk like they do or like they want them to.

Up until I was seven years old, we lived in one of the most diverse areas in Florida. During those early years, my parents lived near the University of Florida campus, where they were both completing graduate school. Our apartment complex was filled with international students and families, and my best friend was a fun-loving European girl about my age. The school I attended was an equally diverse Christian academy, and we all lived in this melting pot of cultural differences that blended together to form a close-knit family.

It wasn't until we moved to the South, which is identified as those states south of the Mason-Dixon Line (except for Florida with its diverse heritage), that I was introduced to racial tensions. During the summer of 1992, my father accepted a position as a professor of counseling at the University of Alabama. Our family of four-soon-to-be-five—my parents, five-year-old Lou, baby Julius in the womb, and me—moved to Alabama prior to the new school year.

Alabama was a fun, new adventure. It was our first time moving as a family, and though I was very shy, I was curious about what this new place had to offer. When we arrived at school on the first day, I remember a class full of eager, curious kids who found me to be an interesting newcomer. I didn't realize this at the time, but we were one of the only minority families in the school. It was my second-grade year. We were all full of insight, growing intellect, and, for some, a burgeoning entrepreneurial spirit. One of my new friends started a lucrative mechanical-pencil-selling business. Since mechanical pencils were considered a luxury, any second-grader with a surplus of cash that was intended for lunch money would forfeit at least one or two dollars for the highly esteemed mechanical pencils.

Burgeoning entrepreneur I was not, but scholastic athlete I was. On day one, I started to stand out in my classes for my intellect and on the playground for my strength and dexterity. Both of my parents were focused on driving our education and introducing us to healthy activities, like sports. They wanted to ensure we had every door open to us. My parents started teaching my siblings and me how to read at three years old, and by the time we were five, we were reading more mature books. While I still loved the simplicity of colors, counting, and rhyming through Dr. Seuss, by five years old I was also learning about the dizzying world of love and romance through Jane Austen's *Pride and Prejudice*. It probably explains my penchant for Nora Roberts and Jasmine Guillory romance novels.

I had also been introduced to a variety of sports, and by the time we moved to Alabama, I showed talent and skills for softball, basketball, and gymnastics. My tennis career, on the other hand, sadly began and ended at three years old. My dad, a semiprofessional tennis player, was eager to share his love for the game with his less-than-enthusiastic firstborn. I had a pink tennis skirt and a blue child's tennis racket that was strangely bigger than my whole body. After several shocking moments with a ball machine whizzing balls past my face, I stormed off the tennis court into my mother's arms and retired from tennis within thirty minutes of starting.

Throughout my approximately four years in Alabama, I was at the top of my class, a star softball player, an aggressively efficient basketball player (I fouled out every game; I'm not ashamed), and a determined, easily excited gymnast. Some of my teachers were impressed with my intellect and started sharing more difficult material with me during our after-school programs. With my parents' schedules, we were always the last kids to be picked up from the after-school program. It never bothered me because it meant I could play with my friends longer. Once I reached third grade, the principal's wife, who was also one of the high school math teachers, asked me to come to her classroom after school, where she slowly introduced more complex math principles, such as algebra and trigonometry, two math subjects that I still love. She saw immediate potential in my abilities and wanted to groom them.

Other teachers were not as inclined to groom a child whom they were less than pleased with having in their class. In my fifth-grade year, I had a teacher who never overtly inhibited my intellectual growth, but she also never supported it. Every time I raised my hand to answer a question, she audibly sighed, rolled her eyes, and looked for another child's hand. I remember her body language making me feel embarrassed for even putting my hand up, and I just assumed someone else was better able to answer the question.

This same teacher would tell me I asked too many questions, which was confusing to me because I hated talking in class. Although I loved learning, I was still very shy and introverted, and I only asked questions if I truly couldn't figure something out on my own.

While this teacher was not my favorite, I had a strict respect for authority, and I never thought to question her behavior.

One of the most embarrassing moments was when I went through what I consider my one and only growth spurt. I was ten years old, and it was the year I would almost reach my full height potential. While I currently stand at an intimidating five feet three and a half inches (do not ever forget the half inch), I had just reached five feet even. My favorite pair of sunflower shorts and matching top did not grow with me. While they were now shorter than normal, they weren't short enough that my parents, who were always conservative with our dress code, would keep me from wearing them to school. This teacher, however, thought differently.

As soon as I walked into the classroom, she ushered me out and down the stairs to call my parents. She was adamant about not letting me back in the classroom until I had more appropriate clothing. I felt so ashamed. I didn't want to go back into the classroom for fear that the other kids had heard her chastising me for something I couldn't control. I remember my parents soothing me and having a conversation with the teacher, but that outfit would never reappear in my childhood years.

(Though we retired my favorite sunflower outfit shortly after that day, many years later it would make a surprise and brief appearance at a college Halloween party. After lots of alcohol and a raucous dancing event, the sunflower outfit went into permanent retirement.)

Throughout school, my siblings and I had a knack for making friends and building relationships. I especially made friends with a lot of the little boys, mainly because it was just me and my brothers for most of my elementary life. The boys at school loved hanging out with me because I liked getting dirty and playing sports, and I was just as strong, if not stronger, than they were. One or two of the little girls who had started to see boys much differently than I did were not impressed with my new friend status with their "play boyfriends." I didn't notice it then, but as an adult I am able to reflect and see their jealousy.

The little girls would play with me when it was just us girls, but the minute the boys came over, they would walk away in a huff. I always thought they just didn't want to get dirty, but it was clear they didn't like how much the boys liked playing with me. One day (again, in fifth grade), the girls apparently decided they were done letting me take over their play boyfriends. Most of the girls decided we should play house, the game where little girls pretend to be mommies, little boys pretend to be daddies, and anyone left over pretends to be the kids in the family. (While the concept of traditional "house" may seem antiquated, remember this was the nineties.)

While we were preparing for this game, one of my best friends said he wanted to be Daddy and he wanted me to be Mommy. We knew it was the right choice because we had recently found out we were two of the fastest kids in our grade, so our marriage was completely aligned with our athletic prowess. As soon as he said that he wanted me to be Mommy with him, a girl who had been one of my best friends immediately yelled out, "You can't play house. You're the wrong color." My soon-to-be husband looked at me and my used-to-be friend in confusion and said, "That doesn't even make sense." When the little girl argued that if I played no one else could play, I, as one who never wanted to be the center of attention, left the game in tears.

I immediately ran to my teacher, who had already showed disdain for me. Trying to hold back the tears, I looked up into her blue eyes and pale skin, and told her, "She said I was the wrong color to play house." My teacher, in her infinite wisdom, said, "She's right. You are the wrong color, so you shouldn't play." I remember being astonished and devastated. I ran down the hill from the outdoor playground and into the back door that led to our classroom. I don't remember much about the rest of that day. I do remember a very important conversation with my parents that night.

That was the night I learned about race, racial injustice, and ignorance. It's "the talk" that most black and minority parents have with their children right around this age, if not sooner. My parents explained that some people in this world would discriminate against me simply because of the color of my skin, people who didn't understand or care how beautiful, smart, and amazing I was, and that those people might hurt my feelings. They explained that even if people hurt my feelings, it didn't mean they were right. They instilled in me the belief that ignorance and fear do not define me. They didn't try to sugarcoat what was going on. They were honest and open about how the world may look at someone different than themselves, especially a little black girl.

From that moment on, I was exposed to a lot of racial-history shows, education, and stories from my own parents' lives. I learned about Maya Angelou's painful journey and remarkable wisdom, Harriet Tubman's fierce determination, Sojourner Truth's strength and impenetrable pride, George Washington Carver's genius and determination. They helped me realize the beauty that was in my skin, in my history, in my family, and in me. When I was told I was black because I had been burned in a fire, I was too dark for anyone to like me, I was disgusting, or when derogatory terms were yelled at me, I would always remember the words and knowledge my parents imparted to me. As the civil rights activist and poet Maya Angelou said in her poem of the same name, "Still I rise."

In 1996 we moved from Alabama to North Carolina. By the time we moved, I'd had the mixed experiences of being selected for lead opportunities in school plays and on sports teams to being discriminated against and cast down because I didn't look the part. I didn't quite learn how to stand up for myself in Alabama, but I did learn that people looked at me differently and that I didn't have to listen to them.

My parents had thrived in Alabama. They had a great social network and rewarding careers, and they found the balance they needed as thirty-something, professional parents in a community of like-minded people. When I talk to my parents about our time in Alabama, they say they loved living there. Recently, I specifically asked them, "Why did you enjoy living during such a terrible time?" They explained that, as adults, they'd had true friends and true enemies. While, as a kid, racial discrimination was new and shocking to me, they had already survived a lifetime full of it. In Alabama, the people who discriminated against them were open and honest about it, so they never had to guess. They knew that other people's ignorance wasn't their ignorance, so why entertain it?

The older I became, the better I understood my parents' mind-set. Throughout middle and high school, I began to break out of my shell, especially after I started competing in pageants at twelve years old. I was exposed to a more adult world, one in which people feared who I was and what I represented: an intelligent, determined, young black girl who knew what ignorance was and chose not to accept it. There were also people who not only accepted what I brought to a whitewashed environment, they loved it and encouraged me to thrive in it.

I remember one specific pageant coach who sought me out early on in my pageant career. We didn't have money or connections like my non-black counterparts, but we did have a wonderful mentor who watched me on stage and knew I had something special. He worked at a pageant store, and he graciously let me borrow gowns, coached me on pageant etiquette, and became a dear, wonderful mentor from my childhood throughout my adult life.

During my ninth-grade year I became one of the youngest and one of only two black women to win my high school pageant, a privilege that was typically reserved for seniors and never for minorities. Winning that pageant opened the door for the other black winner, who came several years after me.

I started to stand up for myself in a different way, sometimes with anger, sometimes with arrogance, sometimes with wit and humor, and sometimes with a quiet look. I was trying to figure out what my race meant to me. To further complicate matters, I was no longer just experiencing discrimination from those who looked different than me, but from my own peers: young black girls just like me. My clothes and the fact that I was a cheerleader and the student body president made them think I was trying to show off, that I wasn't black enough, that I didn't speak like them.

For a while, I wanted to fit in with them. I would find a way to go to their parties, and if I dated one of the "brothas" at school, I had a temporary "in" until the inevitable breakup. They made me feel as though I wasn't black enough. I had no problem with the way they talked or the way they looked. I did have a problem with them rolling their eyes every time they saw me. It took years of trying to fit in with this crowd throughout middle school and high school for me to realize that just because I wasn't like them didn't mean I wasn't the perfect version of me. Though I struggled with insecurities from my own racial group, I was determined not to let others feel those same insecurities because they looked or acted different.

I would take that understanding with me beyond high school, beyond college, and into my adult life.

At the beginning of my consulting career, I was assessing an organization whose patients were saying that they were experiencing poor customer service. The chief executive officer (CEO) had never met me in person or over the phone and only knew me by my given name, Kristian Tobias, which is often confused with a Jewish boy's name. When I arrived onsite at this organization, as usual, I immediately befriended whomever I encountered, especially the CEO's secretary. When the CEO came out to greet "Kristian Tobias," he didn't deign to look in my direction and frustratedly asked his now-horrified secretary, "Where is Kristian Tobias?"

As she tried to explain that the young black woman in front of him was Kristian Tobias, I stepped forward, smiled, grabbed his hand, and said, "It's a pleasure to meet you. I'm Kristian Tobias. Shall we talk in your office about your top priorities?" You would think he would have been embarrassed. Instead, he became even more frustrated and, dare I say, offended that I would mislead him in such a deceitful way.

Within the first five seconds after he reluctantly let me into his office and sat down with me, he informed me that he didn't think I could do anything for him and his organization. As any smart consultant would do, I had done my research on this struggling business. The metrics that measured how patients perceived their experiences were abysmal at best, and their own employees were disgruntled and angry. So I asked him the question I ask every single one of my clients: "What are some of the things your patients are saying about their experiences?" When he quickly answered that things were fine and their patients were fine, I calmly and unhurriedly pulled out a stack of metrics completely disproving his feedback. I gave him about two minutes to review the results and allowed silence to loom in the air. Then I did what I do best: I talked to him about the impact of the patient experience in my life. I told him the story about my first two patients I worked with when I first started out as a CNA. I explained to him the impact that I've been able to make in my brief yet powerful work in consulting and talked to him about how the data speaks volumes, but the patients' stories are the reason we do what we do.

After about an hour in his office, he wanted to know more about our work and introduced me to the rest of his team. Despite the fact that he never apologized or even admitted he was wrong in his approach toward me, his organization did take our consulting advice and achieved impressive results.

It is not lost on me that there are some people in this world who will never care to appreciate who I am simply because I have dark brown skin. I am also acutely aware that my three-year-old, half-black, half-white niece will endure this same set of trials as she grows up. My goal is to continue striving toward breaking down barriers in a way that makes sense to me. I want to break down the barriers that will allow my niece to achieve greatness and move past the ignorance of those who try to stop her.

I learned that I can gain more traction through listening and a calm resolve than through anger and quick words. Does that mean I don't get offended and defensive and sometimes lash out at an ignorant person? Absolutely not! Just last year I had a heated conversation with a former friend that ended in the dissolution of that relationship. Do I regret my approach to that situation? Absolutely not! Do I wish we could have resolved things and seen eye to eye? I honestly don't know. I can't change someone else's cultural background, and I can't change what they were taught to think. I have always understood that my race is a part of me. I am proud of me, I am proud of who I am, I am proud of being a black woman. I have experiences that can be shared with others and some that cannot. Through it all, I am enough exactly as I am.

You are, too.

TEN

Just Because It's Your Dream Doesn't Mean It's Perfect

Once I finally got my act together in my midtwenties, I realized I didn't just want to work in healthcare organizations, I wanted to provide expert consultation and coaching on people and leadership development as well as business optimization. I wanted to partner with organizations to support their goals and help drive them to the next level of success. I saw all the things that were going on in the inner workings of an organization, and I wanted to analyze and find ways not just to fix them but to help other people understand how they could implement their own long-term fixes for a much greater reward.

Sounds like a daunting goal, doesn't it? Welcome to life inside the head of Kristie. I am a fixer by nature, which is both a benefit and a fault. My passion for fixing, or as I like to call it, "optimizing," organizations would be the right direction to healthily channel my inner Marie Kondo!

People always ask me, "How did you become so successful?" Success is personal, so I always cringe at this question. My success looks different than your success. I can only share what brought me to where I am. I spent a lot of my life saying no to a lot of opportunities because I was scared of failure. I didn't want to rock the boat of perfection. My ability to say yes didn't just happen. It took a lifetime of realizing that saying no was only resulting in me racking up more and more regrets. I found myself living a shell of a life because I was afraid of not being perfect, looking perfect, or sounding perfect.

When I was diagnosed with PTSD, the trauma resulted in a lot of memory loss and a lot of blocking out the person I used to be prior to my diagnosis. For the first three to five years after my diagnosis, this memory loss pissed me off and increased my erratic and suicidal behaviors. But the blessing in disguise was I started the slow, painful process of healing. I also opened myself up to embracing and moving past all the fear that pushed me to say no. I realized that being in the darkest part of my mind was far scarier than anything the world could throw at me, so I metaphorically started a new life in which I embraced the yes to steadily remove the darkness.

Throughout this time of personal transition, I spent four years working alongside one of the hardest-working businessmen I have ever met. He became and still is a mentor and friend whom I am grateful to have in my life. We worked side by side to relentlessly build the operations, finance, human resources, and training and development sides of his three healthcare and fitness start-ups.

During those four years, I attended graduate school part-time to supplement my knowledge base. As part of my master's program, I wrote a thesis on the patient-focused work of the founder of the consulting company I currently work for, and was inspired and energized to understand more of the healthcare consulting world.

After completing my master's degree, I took a risk and left the healthcare and fitness start-ups to take on a year-long postgraduate fellowship that offered no guarantee of a job after its completion. And before you ask the question, no, I didn't have a trust fund, no I didn't have any money in savings, and no I didn't have any other support besides my own money. I took a risk and spent years getting by on an overdrawn bank account, living in a less-than-ideal apartment complex, and subsisting on ramen noodles. I knew that, to achieve my goals, I had to step out on faith and grit and be OK with not being OK.

To say I worked my ass off in that role to prove myself is an understatement. I worked every single job, every single shift, and in every single department in that hospital. Working third shift in the emergency department, then immediately working day shift in the administration department gave me a new understanding of endurance and sleeping while standing up! I made a name for myself, and my driven, ambitious reputation afforded me countless opportunities that provided unparalleled learning opportunities. My work ethic, focus, and blind commitment to excellence eventually led to a human resources and organizational development role in the hospital that helped set me up for success in pursuing a consultant position.

My hospital partnered with what would become the current company I work for, and I quickly befriended our consultant. We had lots of conversations over coffee with me unabashedly asking her about her life and how she became a consultant. She recommended I apply for a position in our data and analytics division that would have me consulting other consultants on metrics that drive success. Even with her as one of my main references, I did not get the position. However, the human resources point of contact (now a dear friend of mine) asked if she could keep my résumé on file, as she thought my values and skills were a good fit for the company, just not in that role.

I was crushed! I knew that working for this company was my calling, but God knew His timing better than I did. That did not stop me from feeling discouraged about this setback in pursuing my dreams.

All of this occurred during the end of my postgraduate fellowship. Prior to this conversation, the hospital I worked for had offered me a position in human resources and organizational development, which I originally turned down in hopes that this consultant role would work out. When I was told I did not get that job, I humbly accepted what would turn into an excellent growth position for me in human resources and organizational development with my hospital.

I learned a lot about humility and grace in my human resources role. I maintained my ambition and drive, but I also layered in a little bit of pride. I received a lot of praise and feedback during my postgraduate fellowship, which was a huge ego boost. I thought I was ready to dominate the human resources world as a stepping-stone to my true dream of being a consultant. I planned on using the experience to pad my résumé, then revisit the company that turned me down for the position in hopes that they would reconsider me for one of their higher-level consulting roles.

As I grew and thrived in that role, I had a director and a manager who served as mentors to help me mature and release my personal pride and move toward collaboration. I have always been really good at getting things done the way I want them to be done. In human resources, however, you have an entire organization with several different departments that operate in a variety of ways that you must consider before making any decisions.

I made one of many mistakes when I pissed off a coworker who worked in the administrative suite that housed our senior-most leaders. She asked me to help her understand her benefits, and after ten minutes of frustration, the call ended abruptly. Seconds later, the director of human resources, also a dear friend and mentor, knocked on my door and asked me about the conversation.

What I thought was me patiently explaining the details of our benefit plan to my coworker was actually me exasperatedly telling her in not so many words, "You are wrong. Please stop calling me." Perspective is everything. I learned the not-so-graceful art of guiding and leading people twice my age with respect and humility. That wouldn't be the last time I was "called to the carpet" for my driven but sometimes overly eager perspective on how things should be done. The positive reactions to me adjusting my approach started to outweigh the negative reactions of my more direct and seemingly abrasive approach. I learned how to control my ever-present and ever-emotive facial expressions, so I could listen more than react to the people I worked with. What I humbly learned was how to support and empower other leaders to succeed instead of making it the Kristie Show.

Exactly one year later, I was contacted by my company, and they asked if I would consider applying for a different position. This newly developed role would have me based in our Pensacola office but travel-ing 50 percent of the time. I would be developing analytical resources, consulting other consultants, and traveling to consult our clients on these resources. After three months of interviews, I was offered the position, and I moved from North Carolina to Pensacola, Florida.

I hit the ground running and said yes to absolutely every oppor-tunity. Six months into my data-analytics consulting role, I was asked if I would consider a promotion to a full-time consultant and national speaker role. I went through a rigorous three months' interview pro-cess, and three months of transition. Then I started the year 2015 in my new dream job as a full-time consultant. Instead of traveling about 50 percent of the time, I was traveling 80 to 85 percent of the time. There were weeks that I would travel Sunday morning through Friday night to consult several clients and catch a speaking gig before returning home to Pensacola. I was a force to be reckoned with. I was also steadily burning the candle at both ends.

After about three years of working at breakneck speed, I burned fully and completely out. I became apathetic and angry, and I found my-self complacently doing my work but not passionately investing in my clients and coworkers. Six months later, after lots of mistakes and very few results, I was asked to leave my current position and apply for a po-sition in another part of the company.

For me, this new position was not only a demotion, it was a huge blow to my living income. After several interviews with different leaders, I was finally offered a position that would be a thirty-thousand-dollar pay cut and a significant step down from my previous role. I was pissed at best. At the time, my live-in boyfriend barely made enough money to buy groceries once a month, so as the sole income provider, I knew that turning this position down was not an option. I gratefully, yet resentfully, took the job.

I started my new position in October 2017, and my first consult-ing project had me spending about a year in New York. Every Monday morning that year, I would fly to LaGuardia Airport in New York and travel to different parts of the city before heading back home on Thursday evenings.

This cosmopolitan New York lifestyle may seem glamorous, but initially I hated this transition. The type of work I was doing took me back to my entry-level data-analytics position, and I felt like no one respected all the hard work and dedication I had put into the company over the past three and a half years. The travel throughout New York was a pain in the ass. Movies glamorize the art of riding the underground metro. The metro station in the movies is in pristine condition with the occasional well-groomed bohemian artists playing a symphony on their violins. Brace yourself for a reality check—this is not real!

The underground metro station smells like piss and death at best. As with many large cities, there is a large homeless population with varying stages of mental illness. As a non–New Yorker and someone who has worked with the homeless ministry in North Carolina, I found myself torn between trying to offer assistance and being terrified because the same person I was trying to help was yelling obscenities at me because of their mental illness.

While the public transportation system is convenient, it requires dexterity and organization. The concept of the "New York minute" is real! It takes exactly sixty seconds for you to miss the one metro that can get you to work exactly on time. It took me about three months to finally figure out how to effectively navigate the metro system. That was the point when I told myself, *I am finally a New Yorker.*

Although I was steadily becoming more comfortable with my ability to fit in as a New Yorker, I was still frustrated with my job. I was actively looking for a way out of this role, and I was also actively ignoring God telling me that this was all part of His plan. After six months of moping, I finally got with the program and really invested in ways I could support this side of the company with my past expertise and analytics background.

While I dreaded going to New York every week, I literally started telling myself, "Girl, you are an adult. Grow the f*ck up and get over it. You have a job, and you get to experience something brand-new that could elevate your career." I had to repeat that mantra to myself every single day. I am not a person who can just have a brand-new attitude because I see the greater good. I am a pouter and a moper. You may never see it, but trust me, in my heart I am a two-year-old child when things seem unfair.

By the time this contract ended and it was time for me to move on to a new contract, I realized two very important things: (1) This demotion was the best thing that could have ever happened to me, and (2) sometimes I can be a royal pain in the ass.

About eighteen months into my position and six months into my newest contract, I was asked if I would consider coming back to my previous $30,000-greater salary in a more complex role on the side of the company I previously worked in. I did not immediately say yes. In fact, I took my time to determine if it was the right choice. I knew the money would be a welcome adjustment, but I didn't want to put myself in the same situation I was in when I burned out and almost missed what became yet another amazing learning opportunity.

In the spring of 2019, I transitioned to what I call a multidimensional opportunity that I would never have been able to have had I not taken what seemed like the deepest cut to my professional career. I am in a position now where I consult in three different areas of the company in a way that elevates my ability and ownership to provide innovative, consultative work to clients and to my colleagues. The president of our entire company knows me by my first name and has sent me personal emails thanking me for my work. I say this not to brag but as a reminder that your plans can sometimes limit you if you block yourself from greater success.

I was so focused on driving faster and faster that when things changed, all I saw was failure. What I didn't see was that as I was changing so was the company, and that transition and timing were what saved my career and improved my ability to make a difference in so many other organizations and people's lives.

Just because you have a dream and a goal and you can see your finish line does not mean it is the actual finish line.

We all find ourselves struggling or in a place where we feel like we are making forward movement; then one misstep, one unfair slight, or one just absolute failure leads us in a completely different direction. This new direction may be the direction to even greater success, so don't miss out on it by being grumpy, pouting, or becoming upset. Give yourself a chance to grieve because you must be honest with your feelings. Then challenge yourself to fight to the next level. Use this transition to push yourself beyond the self-imposing limitations you set. Greatness is realized through dexterity, flexibility, and innovation.

Don't miss out on your greatness because you're focused on what you see as a failure, when it may actually be a blessing and growth opportunity propelling you to far greater success than even you can imagine.

ELEVEN

Don't Defeat Yourself with Your Own Attitude

One of the most enlightening but frustrating parts of my life is traveling almost every single week for work. For the past six years, I have lived out of a suitcase at minimum Mondays through Thursdays. I have spent months traveling on two planes a day from Florida to California to Oregon to Texas to Ohio to North Carolina and back to Florida, all in one week. I maxed out flying on ten planes in one week! I have also spent months traveling to different cities and living a full week in each location. I am best friends with the TSA precheck agents in the Pensacola airport and in certain frequently visited airports, like LaGuardia (LGA) and Dallas/Fort Worth (DFW). (Extra points if you can guess the Pensacola airport code!)

During a trip earlier this year, a colleague and I were on the same flight from Pensacola and happened to arrive at the airport at the same time. As we were walking through the precheck line, I provided my typical greeting to the TSA officers who scanned our IDs, our luggage, and our bodies. As the agents and I discussed our personal lives and weekend plans, I turned to my colleague, who travels almost as much as, if not more than, I do, and he was staring at me with the most curious "Who are you?" look on his face. He said, "Do you go anywhere without making friends?" I just laughed, and the TSA agents all nodded their heads that, yes, I do make friends everywhere.

Traveling is a strategic art, and being a friendly or, at the very least, an amenable traveler will reward you with more perks and less stress than being an angry, disgruntled traveler. The airport and airline employees are only trying to do their jobs, just like you are, so spewing them with disdain over things they can't handle, like the weather or airplane mechanics, is just rude and unacceptable. I get that you are upset, but do not take it out on the one person who is trying to help you. Yes, their customer service may need some work, but think to yourself that maybe they are projecting exactly the same attitude you are giving to them. OK, I'm coming down from my pedestal.

Just because I do not agree with poor behavior at the airport does not mean I am always perky and friendly in the airport. If I'm up before six in the morning for a flight, I am a bitch. I can't even sugarcoat. I hate myself, I hate you, and I hate you for looking at me. I am absolutely, 100 percent not a morning person.

I have a wonderful, amazing, talkative girlfriend, and for about six months we traveled on the same Monday six a.m. flight. I love her dearly, and typically I am just as talkative as she is. But after about four and a half months of traveling together on this same flight, I started avoiding her. Not only is she a morning person, she is the Susie Sunshine of morning people, asking me deep questions, including advice on her work life and personal relationship, before six in the morning.

For those of you who are not familiar with traveling, you typically should arrive at the airport, even small airports, one hour before your flight is scheduled to depart, so my six a.m. flight required a five a.m. arrival. That five a.m. arrival was usually preceded by a four a.m. wake-up call. My personal definition of early is any time before eight in the morning. At four in the morning, I am a beast of a woman who should be avoided. My mother taught me a long time ago that when I am angry or uncomfortable, my facial expressions alone would terrify Sasquatch. I have learned how to temper my facial expressions and go into the "cone of silence" when I am grumpy, irritated, or awake before eight in the morning.

My Susie Sunshine friend finally picked up on the fact that, as she was talking to me and spewing her rainbows, unicorns, and happiness, I was giving her one-word responses with a pained smile. She looked at me one day and asked, "Are you a morning person?" I all but screamed, "No, I am not!" She apologized profusely and asked me why I had never told her. My response was simple. I told her it was too early for my brain to formulate the words to share how I truly felt. And to be honest, in my grumpy morning brain, I thought she talked so much I couldn't get a word in to tell her to stop talking to me.

A morning person I am not, but a seasoned traveler I am. During my first three years of work as a traveling healthcare consultant, I was overly excited and giddy. I delighted in every takeoff and touchdown, every new city, every sunrise and sunset. I was in a state of euphoria for almost three years, until I hit a state of burnout. Then I spent six months dreading every single flight and every single hotel room, vaguely distinguishing one state from another, and easily confusing the West Coast and East Coast. When I transitioned to my new role on a different side of the company, I was still traveling, but to only one location Mondays through Thursdays instead of multiple locations across the United States.

While this adjustment in travel was a welcome change, I was still on edge and becoming increasingly frustrated with the nomadic life of a road warrior. By definition, a road warrior is anyone who spends more time in an airport, airplane, or even a car than they do in their home or hometown.

This brings us to where I was about three months into my new role. It was January 2018 and Winter Storm Grayson attacked everyone on the Northeast Coast, canceling 100 percent of flights out of LaGuardia that week. Going home was not an option, but I had to make it to Pensacola somehow. My typical flight out Thursday was canceled, and it looked like I wouldn't make it back to Pensacola until at least Sunday, which meant a twenty-four-hour turnaround after an extended stay in New York. I was stressed, to say the absolute least.

When I am highly stressed, my PTSD is on high alert. One of the symptoms that accompanies PTSD is flashback night terrors. These night terrors are not always triggered by environmental or emotional factors; sometimes they simply show up on their own.

For me, reliving the last night with my ex, when I was sexually assaulted, raped, abused, then sent to the hospital via ambulance is my regular flashback night terror. My coping mechanism, which I learned from my parents and my trauma therapist, is to go to my safe place. If you remember, my safe place is the beautiful white sand and clear turquoise ocean of the beach. When I am emotionally in a place where I can't logically bring myself to my safe place, panic sets in and my PTSD symptoms are magnified.

This particular Tuesday night, sleeping was futile, as I was traumatized the whole night by flashback night terrors and the inability to find my safe place. These night terrors happened to be the kind that were not triggered by environmental factors. They just decided to show up unannounced and unwanted.

I had a total of sixty minutes of broken sleep and woke up Wednesday morning to all flights being canceled for Thursday, Friday, and some on Saturday. Apparently, the airport gurus were preparing for the worst. As a precaution, they didn't even wait for the winter weather to hit before canceling all flights that would be impacted by Grayson's predicted landfall Thursday morning.

Flight issues don't typically stress me out. After almost four years of consulting, this was not the worst issue I had encountered. But factor in my lack of sleep and pure physical, mental, and emotional exhaustion from dealing with my PTSD, and I was an anxious and chaotic hot mess! In my head, I was screaming—screaming for something to just go right. I was screaming to go home, screaming to not have to deal with the bullsh*t that is my PTSD, screaming to just be done.

A coworker and I were able to book a flight that Wednesday evening that would get us as far south as South Carolina. She needed to get to Georgia. I needed to get to Florida. Silver lining: where we were going in South Carolina just happened to be where my brother Lou, my adorable niece, and her mom live. It's amazing how God works things out. I would love to tell you I saw the positivity and rainbows, and that everything was going to be just perfectly fine and dandy. However, I was too worn out to see anything but added grief and frustration because I was still hours away from my home and my own bed.

Once we booked our flights, we immediately left the office to head to LaGuardia. We arrived and learned that, after all the weather chaos, the plane we were scheduled to fly on decided to give up the ghost. It was broken, and so was our only hope of getting out of New York and possibly making it to our own beds.

My coworker and I decided we were finished. We had no choice but to find a not-so-comfortable seat at our gate and wait out our next steps. As we were listening to other upset passengers complaining about what to do next, we, ironically enough, became everyone's confidantes and advisors.

As a seasoned traveler, sometimes you just can't help but explain how the airport systems work. You know what else? It's amazing how your spirits lift when you start thinking of someone other than yourself. Now, let me be clear: I did not have a divine and humbling "God moment." I was too tired to think about my situation anymore, and I had a challenging and subtle "God moment." A God moment I didn't even realize was happening until our plane miraculously was fixed. I kid you not—that plane was not supposed to make it out of New York. The amazing gate agents and pilot had run all the way around the airport to find the best mechanics to get us out of there!

As people were excitedly filing in line to board, a couple who had repeatedly reached out to my coworker and me to explain how airports work, and who we, for the most part, thought were super annoying, told me and I quote, "Thank you for helping us. You have handled yourself so well, and you helped us feel better about this."

Cue jaw drop, as I know that is not how I felt. It was at that moment that I learned their story: they were there for the husband's mother's funeral, and on their way to the funeral, the husband realized he was having difficulty walking. They went to a doctor and he was diagnosed with a treatable but debilitating disorder. I talked with him about other healthcare options, and he left that night knowing he didn't have to just succumb to his fate.

When we arrived in South Carolina at one thirty Thursday morning, I was starting to see God's message in all of this. He was quietly and consistently telling me, "Don't miss out on my calling because you're too full of your own sadness and despair." That awakening didn't completely change my attitude because, let's be honest, when you're exhausted you stubbornly hold on to that last little bit of pity party until you just can't hold on to it anymore. Nonetheless, I was oddly excited because I would get to see Lou and spend at least a few hours with him and my niece.

Where I live in Florida is seven and a half hours and four states away from Lou. Dear, sweet, amazing Lou stayed up and waited for my coworker and me to arrive in our rental cars. After what was one of the best night's sleep maybe in my life and a quick bonding moment over a Netflix show with Lou, my niece, and her mom, I finally headed down to Florida.

Usually, I don't take pictures at state lines, I don't blast the music, and I don't really grab a meal on this type of trip, mainly because I am too irritated that work, flights, or Mother Nature has delayed my journey. However, after sleep and Lou's wisdom, encouragement, and reminder that I was doing just fine even if it didn't always feel like it, I was determined to live in this moment. I grabbed breakfast and lunch for the road, blasted the best radio station I could find in South Carolina, and headed out. I took a random picture at each rest stop, stopped and talked to strangers, and turned what was truly a seven-and-a-half-hour trip into about an eight-and-a-half-hour trip, just so I could be part of the moment.

It's important to remember that we can defeat ourselves with our own attitude. We were never called to perfection or even to be kind and friendly at every point in our journey. We were called to be honest and to remember that we are never alone in this world.

Who are you touching in this moment? Who is watching you and seeing something beautiful, helpful, and inspiring in you that you can't see in yourself? When you find yourself at the deepest depths of self-pity and despair, give yourself a "lift me up" mantra that you repeat to yourself until you can pretend to believe it. Lou gave me mine, and I encourage you to use it to help make yours.

"I am doing better than I realize, even if I don't see it."

TWELVE

Moving Forward to Invest in Joy

In the summer of 2006, I was dealing with the immediate legal aftermath of the sexual abuse, rape, and trauma caused by my ex. Following my visit to the hospital, I agreed to undergo police investigation with the prospect of prosecuting my ex.

People always ask why rape victims never come forward. It's bad enough dealing with the personal trauma from being assaulted; it's a whole other trauma having to relive it with police officers and detectives, whose main jobs are to dig into the meat of anything that could have possibly happened to lead up to the traumatic incident.

Weeks following the traumatic night, I underwent a round of interviews with two local detectives who were not the detectives at the scene the last night with my ex. While I found that odd, apparently that was the way this investigation was going to be run. As part of university protocol, Wake Forest also assigned their own detective as my legal advocate. He was a godsend. He was responsible for guiding me through what to expect at each phase of the interview and investigation process. He also explained to me his opinion of the way the investigation was being handled.

When I went in for the interviews with the two detectives, my rape-and-trauma advocate drove me to the police station and stayed with me as solace after. I was sick to my stomach, and unfortunately I was vividly remembering every moment from that night. When the round of questions began, it was clear they had talked to my ex before talking to me. Later, the detective advocate at Wake Forest would share that was not the protocol he would have followed. He would have recommended interviewing the victim prior to the suspect, especially in my specific situation.

The interview was like being attacked all over again. The detectives needed to understand my relationship with my ex from the very beginning, so I shared with them how our relationship started when I was fourteen. They cut me off immediately, told me that my ex said we met when I was eighteen years old, and proceeded to spend most of the interview trying to cross-talk me into admitting that I was lying about when I met my ex. They were especially interested in the fact that I told them the first time he forced me to do anything sexual was when we met in person for the first time when I was fifteen years old.

One of the detectives scoffed at my story, and the other detective stayed quiet. After at least an hour of brutal grilling and telling me I was lying, the detective who scoffed at me left the room to take a break, leaving me with the other detective, who had become mysteriously silent. After what seemed like hours, but was only about ten minutes, the silent detective turned to me and asked, "Why didn't you tell anyone that he forced you to do something sexual? If you were my daughter, I would have killed him." Sheepishly, I told him, "I thought that's what you did with your boyfriend." His silence and look of shame and anger were the confirmation I needed to know that, regardless of the outcome, the night was real, the trauma was real, and no matter how many times the other detective tried to push a story that was not true at me, I knew that my story happened, not only to me but, I am certain, to others.

When you are berated by someone trying to convince you to deny a story that you will never forget, you find yourself battling against pretending it never happened and acknowledging the truth. I went in for questioning in February, and I didn't receive a response about the prosecution until a couple of weeks after my birthday, in June, about one month after returning from Russia. The police department called and told me there wasn't enough evidence to prosecute. That news set off another stream of frustration and arguments when I shared it with my parents, concluding with my dad looking me in the eye and saying if I wanted to move forward, he would support me, but that I should know it would be a hard road. I talked with the detective advocate from the university, and he voiced the honest difficulty and likely negative end result of continuing to move forward with a prosecution attempt. While he fully supported justice and personally would have helped support my next steps, I realized I couldn't keep going through this anymore. I decided to close the prosecution attempt.

There was a sense of relief and sorrow with this decision. I couldn't fathom going through yet another interview, being grilled about my horrible relationship and traumatic events. I also hated myself for not being able to speak up about what my ex did to me, to try to prevent someone else from becoming a victim as well. I was angry and sad and confused. I wanted to wallow in that moment and hide behind everything, but I knew that wasn't an option if I wanted to move forward.

Though I couldn't prosecute my ex, the prosecution attempt, regardless of who he sweet-talked into believing him, might have been enough to cause him to think twice about acting on another woman or child again. I can't control him and the decisions he makes, but I can control how I move forward with advocating for those who can't advocate for themselves. The more often I tell my story, the more others will be able to relate and tell their stories to keep this from happening to someone else.

People often make the mistake of saying you have to move on from grief, or you have to move on from the trauma. You never move on from it. That's not possible, nor is it healthy. Moving on implies that it didn't happen and you forget it. Moving on requires you to pretend like the trauma was a one-time situation and that the remnants of it don't live with you forever. Moving forward implies that you acknowledge the pain, but you move toward healing and growth. Moving forward allows you to give others the hope and support they need to also heal.

Moving forward also requires you to remember that your life doesn't stop because of the trauma. Shortly after receiving the news about not having enough evidence to prosecute, I embarked on yet another life-changing journey abroad, to Kenya. Around the same time that I applied to go on the trip to Russia hosted by my university, I also applied for a scholarship to join an organization that works with the HIV/AIDS crisis, on their annual trip to Kenya. I was one of three students from my university selected to receive the scholarship that would afford me the opportunity to go on this trip.

The purpose of the trip was twofold. The organization builds orphanages specifically for children who are HIV positive, and they also actively provide education and awareness about the HIV/AIDS crisis in Kenya and in the United States. Personally, this trip was an opportunity for me to step into an entirely different life perspective and learn new coping tools to help me continue along my path of growth and healing.

Our group traveling to Kenya was comprised of students from universities across North Carolina. We spent one month volunteering in the orphanages in several different cities in Kenya. We also hosted panel discussions with members of parliament and awareness events focused on open, collaborative conversations with Kenyan and American university students on how we could actively focus on educating and spreading awareness about HIV/AIDS.

I made lifelong friends on this trip and learned lessons I couldn't have learned at any other time, in any other place. One of my most memorable experiences was working in part of an orphanage in Kisumu, Kenya, called the family unit. As a reminder, all of these orphanages were for children who were HIV positive. The family unit was specifically designed for children who were two years old or older and still HIV positive.

Allow me to share with you a little bit of biology on how HIV works in the body: At birth, an infected mother can transmit the HIV antibody to the infant. If treatment is started at birth, the HIV antibody has a higher likelihood of converting from being detectable in the bloodstream to not being detectable. This conversion typically occurs by the time a child is two years old. Otherwise, there is a very low likelihood that the conversion will occur, and the child will remain HIV positive.

In an orphanage, being HIV positive reduces your likelihood of being adopted, and the older the child, the lower his or her likelihood of adoption. The family unit was a very special place for this reason. I loved working in it. The children were two to three years old, full of life, excitement, and an insatiable desire to learn everything around them. I became especially close with the nurses and staff in the unit. While I split my time equally between an orphanage in Nairobi and one in Kisumu, the bond in the Kisumu family unit connected and engaged my heart.

I befriended one of the staff members, whom I will call Angel. Angel loved the kids in the unit with her whole heart. She had a son of her own, and I know how much her son was loved by the love she shared with the children in the family unit. Angel and I had endless conversations, and we maintained contact after I left Kenya. Angel taught me grace for others and for myself. I never told her the story of what happened to me. After hearing the story of her life, the hardships she endured, the uphill battle she had every day just to make it to work and take care of her son, I didn't dare complain about anything in my life.

The amazing thing about Angel and really all the people I met in Kenya was the inherent joy and love they shared with everyone. I remember attending a worship service with Angel and a few other members of my group, and I thought the walls were going to blow completely off the tiny worship building with the excitement and enthusiasm that enveloped it. There was something contagious in the way my Kenyan friends embraced every moment of their lives, their work, their worship, their friendships.

It was on that trip that I came to terms with a lot of my own inherent qualities that were present with or without PTSD. Joy was something that I wouldn't say I ever truly embraced or possessed. I was more worried than joyful in my life. I wasn't at peace with myself because I knew I wasn't perfect, but that's never been what life is about. With PTSD, I felt dirty and destroyed. I felt brokenness more than I felt the freedom of being released from a relationship that was filled with abuse and fear. In Kenya, I found myself diving into the lives of my new friends and trying to understand how they could feel so much joy on such a regular basis amid hardships.

I realized I couldn't compare my life to theirs, but instead I should try to understand their joy. Angel said that the simplicity of having air in your lungs, the ability to walk and move to wherever you need to go, and being able to see life and light in the eyes of the children around us were what brought her joy. She openly admitted that joy doesn't mean happiness. Life is hard, and difficulties can be fleeting, but joy has to come from within.

While in Kenya, I visited the slums of Kibera, had my first taste of whiskey with members of parliament, went on safari in Masai Mara, and danced with the Masai men. I also learned the history and depths of African culture and that, as a black woman living in America, understanding the roots of being an African is even more important. I was guided around the impact of the term *African*. As an African, much like Jamaicans, you know everything about your ancestors—what time of day they were born, what tribe they were born to, and the exact location of their births. In America, historically, black men and women were brought over from Africa during the slave trade, and they lost the ability to know the depths of their African culture. It's an eye-opening experience to come to terms with the strength and power in the term *African* and the culture surrounding it. While not all black Americans are African, there is a cultural bond that comes from embracing the beauty of the African culture and its impact on our society.

There is a unity that comes from being part of a country that is so open to embracing and investing in living with joy. My time in Kenya taught me how to embrace grace within myself, the grace to not be OK, the grace to allow joy into my life even when life is hard, unfair, or painful. Joy means knowing that deep within there is a beauty that you possess that unites you with others who may or may not share your story but do share the need to have grace and build joy within themselves.

THIRTEEN

I Embrace Me

If you're a competitive person, a certain level of dedication and commitment is a perpetual part of your life.

Growing up, my siblings and I always competed in sporting events. Even now, as adults, we purposefully stay active. My brother Julius has taken that commitment to activity to a whole other level by playing minor league baseball for the Boston Red Sox!

On top of attending school, an athlete spends hours after school in practices or at games. My main sports were softball and cheerleading. While I officially ended my softball career at fifteen years old, I cheered from middle school through my junior year in undergraduate. Though there are always naysayers who question the validity of the sport of cheerleading, I respond with my own question: "Have you ever cheered?" If you haven't, then I challenge you to spend a day in the life of a college cheerleader, and no, I don't mean at a football game. I mean at the hours of practices prior to football games, where we literally break our backs, necks, and all other body parts to prepare for a game that only lasts a couple of hours.

Speaking of breaking backs, when I was fourteen years old, my stunt group (a group trained to toss tiny girls in the air and miraculously catch them) threw one of our flyers (the tiny girl) just a little too high; she overcompensated and managed to land on the base of my neck. The awkward landing tore all the muscles, ligaments, and tendons in my back. I was supposed to be out of commission for easily one month, but after a doctor prescribed muscle relaxers, Vicodin, and about a week of rest, I was tentatively cleared to return to cheering with my teammates. The long-term impact of that injury resulted in my spending almost eight years with chronic back pain and in perpetual physical therapy. My back didn't fully heal until I quit cheerleading, but that is the price you pay when you're dedicated to a sport you love.

Being an athlete, and especially a cheerleader, wasn't just something I did; it became part of who I was. As an undergraduate, people knew me as "Kristie the cheerleader." When I quit cheerleading, the only thing I had left to my name was my PTSD and a mediocre grade point average. I took for granted the impact of the years of disciplined workouts and moderately healthy eating. With my new PTSD diagnosis came a heavy antidepressant-antianxiety medication. My body reacted poorly to the combination of a no-longer-strict workout routine and eating schedule and my new medication. Within six months, I gained forty pounds and was steadily losing the muscle definition that had defined me for years.

While I tried to adopt a consistent workout routine to lose the weight, the medication and my horrible-at-best eating habits kept me from losing more than twenty pounds in a year. As someone who has always been naturally muscular, I always dreaded weighing myself. Muscle weighs more than fat, and at my heaviest, I was five feet, three and a half inches tall and weighed close to two hundred pounds. From the outside, no one would have ever considered me heavy, but inside I was devastated. All those years of sports and fitness were gone, replaced by a body I didn't recognize.

I struggled with my weight for the better part of a decade. My biggest issue with my body has always been twofold. Number one: as an athlete I was used to being strong, fast, and in shape. Number two: when

I was growing up competing in pageants, gaining more than five pounds was a travesty. During my three years of college cheerleading, I went on a hiatus from competing in pageants. My time was completely occupied with practices and lots and lots of games. When I quit cheer, I thought it only natural that I return to the pageant world.

My quick return was followed by my quick weight gain. My life experiences as an undergraduate had improved my stage presence and interview skills, and even with the weight gain, I was still being recognized by pageant judges as a top contender. But . . . it was the pageant world in the mid-2000s, where they were constantly looking for the next model, not the next girl with a great personality and an average-sized body.

Nonetheless, I kept competing. Every weekend of my senior year in undergraduate school, while my friends were out watching football games, I was training or competing in a local pageant. I made a commitment to myself a long time ago that once I won a major state pageant, I would retire from competing. I put my everything into competing in every pageant system possible. When I graduated from Wake Forest University, I still had not achieved my goal of winning a state title, so I enlisted help from the experts. I spent every bit of money I was making at my job on a pageant boot camp.

During the boot camp, I learned how to connect better with the pageant judges through a more refined interview approach and more effective stage presence. But the biggest lesson I learned (or so I thought) was how to control my food intake and adjust my workouts to reclaim my pageant body. I targeted my sights on the 2010 Miss North Carolina International pageant and put my all into preparing to compete and hopefully win the title.

As with everything I do, I went full speed ahead, and instead of adhering to my recommended food portions, I cut my intake in half and was eating fewer than a thousand calories per day. I also increased my workout plan to include twice-per-day workouts for no less than one hour each. I was burning a minimum of two thousand calories per day. I accelerated my preparation for the pageant about sixty days prior to competition day. By the thirtieth day of intensive preparation, I had dropped fifteen to twenty pounds. I was subsisting on one can of tuna, a glass of orange juice, and, when I really became desperate, a tablespoon of peanut butter three times per day. My boyfriend at the time became increasingly worried about my obsession to prepare for Miss North Carolina International, and it would take his persistence to bring me back from a very dangerous place.

I was moody and a real delight to be around. Have you ever been around someone who hasn't eaten carbs or normal food in weeks? It's not pretty! When I blacked out in my boyfriend's arms while walking to the car from a pool party, we both knew it was time for a change before something more serious happened. He threatened to tell my parents if I didn't start eating real food. I had been playing a dangerous game with my health. It's easy to take for granted the impact drastic decisions have on our lives until we see the physical effects. Waking up on the ground in the parking lot, cradled by my boyfriend, and staring into his terrified face was my wake-up call.

I backed off my self-imposed nutrition plan and incorporated healthier, longer-lasting food items, like greens, sweet potatoes, and lean protein. I also moved to one workout per day for about an hour and a half, but listened to my body when it needed a break. I incorporated one rest day per week. I walked into the Miss North Carolina International Pageant about ten pounds heavier than I intended, and won almost every phase of competition, and . . . wait for it . . . the title! I was Miss North Carolina International 2010! When I competed in the Miss International Pageant about six months later, I competed at a healthier, slightly heavier weight with a much better disposition due to the eating of carbs and placed fourth runner-up. Texas won that year—Texas always wins.

After completing my year of service as Miss North Carolina International, at the experienced age of twenty-four, I retired from the pageant world. It was no longer a healthy outlet for me. It was becoming an obsession with my body. Now, before you blame all of this on pageants, yes, I know there is an outdated perspective on beauty, but that's not just the pageant world; that's many parts of society. The pageant world was one of the few places I felt empowered and connected to women just like me. I built lifelong friendships from my time competing. I retired because I personally was approaching competition in a way that no longer allowed me to feel that empowerment.

From my time competing and reigning as Miss North Carolina International, I learned how to connect with people of all ages, socioeconomic backgrounds, political views, ethnicities, races, and opinions. I was a role model for men and women, but especially young, impressionable girls, and I took that responsibility very seriously. I didn't want them to doubt who they are because society, their friends, or even their families tell them they are not enough. I wanted them to know they are always enough and that they should always embrace the unique person God created them to be. I learned the simple art of embracing me and teaching others to embrace themselves.

Embracing yourself and your authenticity takes consistent work. It's a dynamic art that doesn't come from just saying, "I am enough," or "I embrace me." It takes putting in the effort to train your mind and your heart to know that even on the bad days, the days when you feel anxiety building and depression setting in, you must make the choice to embrace yourself.

Even now, I look in the mirror and see that extra back roll that I swear was not there earlier in the day, or the fact that my legs not only touch, they happily rub together and chafe at the most inopportune times, and I think, *Wow! How did I let myself get this way?* I forcefully tell myself, *Girl, you are not perfect. You are the perfect version of the person God created you to be. You are enough. You are the only person who can achieve the purpose God has set out for you.* This self-acceptance and self-healing statement do not work immediately. It takes repetition, but when I allow my mind to think the positive affirmation of embracing exactly who I am, my mind and my heart become trained in accepting those positive affirmations.

In 2016, I put that positive affirmation to the test. Yet again, I found myself inching closer to two hundred pounds. I had been traveling as a consultant for about a year and a half, and I realized I needed a boost to restart my self-discipline. I reached out to a friend who owned his own fitness business, and he connected me with a trainer at a local gym who would become one of my closest friends as well as one of my spiritual confidantes. After lots of conversations on my health and fitness goals, we decided that I would compete in a bodybuilding competition.

For a little education, bodybuilding competitions have several different categories for men and women. In the female divisions, there are bikini, figure, physique, and bodybuilding categories. In the simplest terms, from bikini to bodybuilding, the criteria to compete includes increasing or more defined muscle dimensions.

My trainer and I both agreed that, with my musculature, the figure category was the best fit. Before we could start training, I had to set a mental and spiritual goal for why I was training. I couldn't allow myself to revert to my old habit of training just to look good. I knew I was no longer disciplined, not just physically but also in my mind and my heart. I was exhausted and losing the focus and motivation I needed to excel at my work and, really, my life. Training with my new trainer was more than just training for physical outcomes, it was training for an overall better sense of self.

We embarked on a four-month journey that included a healthier eating plan, incorporating foods that fed my body and my mind. We focused on workout routines that I could do at the gym while home and in my hotel room or even outside when on the road. We also worked on my tendency to overdo it by focusing on pacing myself and giving myself grace. One night after a disastrous travel day, I had worked all day and jumped on a severely delayed evening flight only to land in my next work destination at one in the morning. I was supposed to be up by four a.m. to train for about an hour and a half before going in for another full day of client meetings. I went into my hotel room that night, sat on my bed, and just broke down. I was exhausted and I was frustrated. I immediately texted my trainer, who by the grace of God just happened to be up, and she called me. She said in no uncertain terms, "Go to sleep and try again tomorrow. You do not have to kill yourself, but you do have to take care of yourself." It was the missing piece to my self-acceptance journey: grace.

My trainer was very serious about my focus on extending grace to myself. While we had originally targeted a competition in October of 2016, four months after we started training in July, she told me that if she didn't think I was ready, we would move my competition date out further, to another competition. The fact that the pressure was off, and all I needed to focus on was healthily training my mind, my heart, and my body, accelerated my progress toward being competition-ready. I competed in October and won three medals! I was excited because I knew that, no matter what the judges or other people thought about my body, I was fulfilled with my new perspective on having a healthy mind-set about my life.

While I did not maintain my competition figure, I did maintain the healthy art of instilling grace in my life. I am now about thirty, maybe even forty pounds heavier than when I competed. I honestly only know my weight from my annual doctor's appointments because one thing my trainer taught me was to stop looking at the scale and start paying attention to how I feel. I literally never weigh myself. I also don't consistently eat the prescribed nutrition plan from my competition days. I focus on moderating my overall food intake and eating to fuel my body, not just because food is around. I enjoy a glass of wine, a piece of cake, pizza, pasta, and other foods all the so-called diets tell you not to eat. I know I feel physically, mentally, and spiritually healthier when I eat longer-lasting, fuel-focused foods, like sweet potatoes, lean meats, and lots of green vegetables.

Ultimately, it's about me and what my body, my heart, and my soul need. It's about extending grace to enjoy life without being imprisoned by my decisions. The grace to embrace me and all of me, not just the me that happened to work out today or happened to eat super healthy today. It's embracing the me that also had a glass or two of wine and enjoyed time chatting with girlfriends. It's embracing the me who chose six hours of sleep over working out at five in the morning.

Now is your time to focus on your self-acceptance journey. What decisions have you made that are imprisoning you and keeping you from embracing yourself? How are you allowing social media or even people in your life to tell you what you should look like or how you should feel? Embracing yourself is a continuous journey, and it starts with releasing the idea that you don't deserve grace, that you must look a certain way to be loved, accepted, or perfect. You are the only person who can live out your purpose. Step back from the mirror of self-doubt and self-deprecation. Replace it with words of self-affirmation, strength, and grace.

Embrace you, all of you, and give yourself the grace to enjoy and engage in your life with love and self-acceptance.

FOURTEEN

The Art of Giving a F*ck and Not Letting Other People Be the Guiding Force in Your Life

I would love to be one of those people who can say with confidence and pride, "I do not give a f*ck what you think about me." It must be a treat not to let anyone or anything bring you down. Fun fact: I can count on zero hands how many people I know who actually don't care what people think.

The interesting thing about life is we don't live in isolation. The closest I came to isolation was when I went to Guatemala with Pensacola Habitat for Humanity in April 2015 to build stoves. We were staying at a hotel that had bungalow-style rooms, and I was the only one who came on the trip by myself. While I had friends and also became friends with everyone on the trip, my other half had no interest in going on the trip with me. In fact, the night before I left, a group of my friends in Pensacola took me out for drinks and a final goodbye, since I would be gone for a couple of weeks, but my other half either forgot or didn't care that I was leaving the country and didn't even contact me before I left the next morning. He also failed to take me to the airport, so that was a fun five-in-the-morning Uber ride.

Of all the people I know, I think he comes the closest to not caring what people think about him until it affects him personally. When I happily refused to contact him for most of my time in Guatemala, his not caring what people think about him quickly turned into his realizing he messed up big time, and he needed to do something to make up for it. He did so on my next solo trip abroad, about a year and a half later, when he secretly snuck several very sweet goodbye cards and drawings in my suitcase and . . . drove me to the airport. Talk about progress!

During the Guatemala trip, we were surrounded by people during the day and most of the evening. Then at the end of the day, everyone retired to their rooms with their significant others, family members, or friends and listened to the sounds of nature. The Wi-Fi tended to be spotty, and I made a point a long time ago to try to avoid electronics on big trips, especially trips abroad. Alone in my bungalow, I realized how isolated I was. I have a phobia of being alone. While I need alone time to recharge, if I spend more than a few hours without anyone else around, I physically and emotionally panic.

When I was sitting alone on my bed in Guatemala, listening to the buzzing of a massive horsefly that found my ear especially enticing, I realized that if something happened to me during the night, nobody would know until morning. As panic attempted to set in, I remembered one of the many coping skills I learned in dealing with anxiety and panic attacks: write it down. The act of writing calmed my nerves and connected me with the reality that I was going to be OK, and I was technically surrounded by people, even though in my immediate environment I was alone.

In that isolation, I found myself thinking, *What would people think about me if I have a panic attack in the middle of Guatemala?* Although the coping mechanism of writing helped reduce my panic, I think the realization that I didn't want other people to think I couldn't handle myself on such an impactful trip also calmed my nerves and helped me get hold of myself.

I am a people pleaser by nature. It bothers me when I learn that someone doesn't like me. As a teenager, I pretended to be tough as nails. I used the phrases "I don't care what they think" and "I do what I want" quite often in those days and well into my twenties. I used them as a defense mechanism, especially in conversations with people whose opinions I didn't agree with. I was deathly afraid of our disagreement sparking their poor opinion of me, so I used the art of reverse psychology to pretend I didn't care. Reverse psychology may have made people think I really didn't care, but inside I was battling my inability to control whether or not that person was upset with me or liked me less because I had a different opinion then they did.

Interestingly, while in my thirties my anxiety has lessened when it comes to caring if people like me, I have also become less polarizing by focusing more on trying to understand the people around me. I find it's easier to stop, listen, and discuss than to just pretend I give no f*cks about their opinion.

My mother is one of the people I admire the most. Her resilience and perceived ability to just let things and people's opinions roll off of her shoulders is remarkable and should be revered. As I was writing this chapter, I called her and we had a really great conversation about the reality of caring what people think about you. In talking with her, she said it perfectly: "I know you hear me say, 'I just do me and let other people do them,' but truthfully, to a certain extent, I do care what people think. The difference is I don't let what they think impact the direction I choose to go in my life." Profound statements from my fabulous mother!

So where does this caring what people think stem from, and how do you handle it without letting it control you? It's different for everyone. I have some friends who are truly terrified of not having people like them. They equate being liked to the highest form of worth and value. For me, it comes from my need for perfection, which never truly went away. Competing in pageants, during your interview you could be asked such controversial questions as, "What are your feelings on abortion?" or "What are your thoughts on gun control?" Those questions can result in answers that may truly upset someone. What any good pageant interview coach will teach you is to choose a side. It doesn't have to be the right side; you just need to be able to speak eloquently and confidently about that side.

Something else I learned from life and pageant coaching was how to read the room. I trained myself to always know both sides of any polarizing situation, so I could speak to one side or the other on stage or in a debate with strangers at a bar. Being able to speak on just about any political, socioeconomic, or race-oriented topic in a way that engages and does not polarize is an art. It's an art I really didn't come close to understanding and to some extent get the hang of until my thirties.

I am a passionate person, especially when it comes to topics I care deeply about. When that passion comes out, I am determined to get my point across, even to the point of rudely interrupting the person I am talking to. The problem with that is the minute I feel myself getting heated, my panic sets in because I know I am about to offend someone, and they may potentially not like me.

When I hit thirty, a switch turned on, a switch to something I call patience and tact. I learned that, while caring what people think about me is never going to go away, I can control the panic I feel by thinking about other people instead of just myself, especially in sensitive conversations. If I know I am passionate about my point of view and I feel like the conversation is becoming heated, it is most likely because the person I am talking to is also passionate about his or her point of view.

Did you know it is possible to not say a word when someone else is talking, even if you disagree with that person? I know—it's mind boggling to me, too, but it is possible. I had to learn physical techniques to help me stop before speaking. I learned the simple art of "the pause"; that is, instead of saying what you want to say in the heat of the moment, you pause, breathe, and let the other person finish their thought. If you have reached the expert level of the pause, you'll find you can pause, let the person finish, and not even think about what you want to say next. That's true mastery of the pause.

Another coping technique I learned and, dare I say, have truly mastered is "the drink" or "the eat." This is one of my favorites, especially if there is wine or something chocolate. When you are tempted to interrupt someone or insert your opinion before you have truly listened to the other person, sip some of your beverage or take a bite of whatever you are eating. When your mouth is occupied, it is significantly harder to provide a retort, so it forces you to stop and, ideally, wait until the other person has finished their thought. Truly mastering the eat or especially the drink involves completely forgetting you are having a conversation and finishing your glass of wine. That's what I call expert status.

While these coping techniques are genius (if I do say so myself), it still doesn't get to what I know you are thinking is the root cause—*How do I stop caring what people think?* Here is the truth: you don't. I know that may not be the answer you were hoping for, but I'm not here to make things easier for you; I'm here to make things realistic for you. What you can do is make caring what people think an art instead of a requirement.

Just because you care about what someone thinks, that does not mean you have to take to heart what someone thinks. You are still in full control of your life, and you, and only you, own the direction you need to go in your life. At the end of the day, someone's opinion of you truly shouldn't have the ability to impact the way you choose to live your life. The question, though, is, how do you choose to live your life? What are your values, your priorities, and your passions? What drives, motivates, and inspires you? What are your absolutes, your must-haves, and your absolutely nevers? Answering these questions will help you identify what's important to you and only you. Though someone else may have similar answers, the uniqueness of your life and your journey will help you truly begin to move forward from the crippling anxiety, such as I once had, of deeply caring and investing in what people think about you.

Realizing that though I may care, I don't have to invest in other people's opinions was like a weight being lifted off of my shoulders. Knowing I can listen, process, and discard opinions that don't meet any of the criteria in my life that will bring me joy and fulfillment is enlightening and a huge relief.

So here is your challenge: Have you set the criteria for your life based on the questions we just noted? Have you identified what you need to bring you purpose and fulfillment, and what you absolutely can't have in your life?

You will not accomplish this all in one sitting, and the answers to these questions may change, but the key is thinking about them and using them to help you truly focus on the art of giving a f*ck but not letting other people's opinions guide how you choose to live your life.

FIFTEEN

Season of Discernment

Most people have a certain level of curiosity with my personal life. Apparently, it's fascinating that I have managed to remain single and childless at the age of thirty-four. When I tell people that my season in life is purposeful, they are typically bewildered by such a crass comment. How dare I say that I am more than happy being single and without a child! It's blasphemy!

Ironically, I don't have any judgement about or problems with anyone who is engaged, married, or has a family. I celebrate their personal and professional life decisions. My friends who know and understand me say, "Girl, stay single as long as you can. You have way too much to do in your life to focus on someone else." They are absolutely right. Though I am in the right stage of my life to not be in a relationship, I am in a season of questionable dating patterns. It's easy to forget about the good times during this season. When I first started writing this chapter, I bitterly wanted to title it "The Season of Scrubs"!

You remember the TLC song "No Scrubs"? The song describes a "scrub" as a man who thinks he has it all going on but isn't willing or able to show that he values the woman he is with. A scrub takes advantage of the woman he is with for his own benefit. The verses in the song describe ways that the scrub acts that are lazy at best.

When I was angrily writing the first draft of this chapter, I had gone through yet another scrub-like encounter and was questioning how these men keep finding me. But . . . I had to remember another telling part of the song, the chorus, which added some truth and reality to my so-called Season of Scrubs.

The chorus speaks to the way a woman who values herself and her own worth should say something very important to the scrub: no. No to letting him have part of your life, take you out, or try to steal your worth. This part of the song should be sung loudly if, and only if, you are approaching your Season of Scrubs in this way.

The chorus provides a huge reality check for me. Not only can I *not* sing that chorus loudly and proudly, but my version of the chorus has included a response to the scrub of yes. Yes, I will let you have part of my valuable time, take me out, and take advantage of my worth.

My Season of Scrubs should really be renamed my Season of Yes.

Near the end of my twenty-ninth year, I started dating a guy who truthfully was never a match for me. He was a fun guy when things were good, but we didn't share the same outlook on life.

If you were to ask him today if we were a match, he would tell you we absolutely were not. We dated for just shy of four tumultuous years. While we made some amazing memories—trips abroad, making dinner together, Valentine's beach celebrations—by the end of the relationship we both walked away defeated and ready for it to be over.

The one good thing that remains from our relationship is our dog Cooper, whom we share custody of. Yes, we share custody of a dog. Judge all you want, but how can you say no to an adorably cute puppy who comes running when you call him and greets you with kisses and hugs?

Reflecting on that relationship, I have to question how it even started. I was about one year into my time in Pensacola. The year prior to moving to Pensacola, my boyfriend at the time and I broke up. He didn't like that I was choosing to advance my career by moving away. While he was a decent guy, he wanted someone who was ready to settle down and help care for him and his child. *Um, excuse me, sir, have you met me?*

While I respect that he knew what he wanted from a relationship, I wasn't the person to offer that, so we mutually decided to part ways. When I moved to Pensacola, I quickly joined several online Meetup groups. Meetup is an online network that creates interest-based groups that meet in person in a safe space. Each Meetup group is aligned with a specific city.

I joined a handful of Meetup groups, and I started meeting all sorts of interesting people around Pensacola. I eventually met a group of women who have become my lifelong friends and have supported and loved me every single day that I have lived in Pensacola.

I also began meeting men in the area and yet again started my casual dating career. As I started testing the waters of dating in my new city and with these new people, I realized I wasn't sure how to discern the type of man I was looking for. All I knew was I wasn't looking for a long-term commitment.

In addition to Meetup, I also joined a couple of dating apps, where I was even less discerning. My criteria to meet up with a man on the dating app was, Did he contact me on the dating app messenger? If the answer was yes, and I felt a physical attraction to him, and he could conduct a somewhat interesting conversation, then I was interested.

I will never put down any of the guys I dated, not even the crazy ones. What I will say is, when you approach dating with a blind and, dare I say, lazy "yes" attitude, well . . . you can't really be surprised when the men you meet aren't a good match.

The irony is, in my twenties in North Carolina, while my discernment was still nowhere near where it needed to be, I nevertheless had standards. I wasn't as quick to spend dedicated time with someone, much less give of myself, until I was sure of our chemistry and that I could trust him.

Except for a handful, the men I dated during that time could be described as givers. They gave fully of themselves to me because I set a standard of that behavior as an expectation. I didn't chase men, or mass text them, or even contact them. Most of the time, I could probably be described as indifferent until a man could prove he was really interested in me.

When I was a twenty-year-old undergraduate, shortly after the chaos of being diagnosed with PTSD, I started dating a beautiful, selfless man whom I will call Nico. Nico was a charmer in the sweetest possible way. He truly knew how to court a college woman. He was in a fraternity that my sorority pledge class had recently started partnering with for parties and date functions.

We attended all of our events together and alternated staying in each other's dorm rooms. He lived in his designated fraternity's dorm. I would frequently wake up, jump down from the cozy top bunk, get dressed, and on my way out of the dorm, say goodbye to the invariable couple of guys still awake from the night before, playing Champong.

By definition, Champong is a game in which opponents face off against each other with a wooden table between them. On each side of the table are Solo cups placed in a diamond shape, filled a quarter of the way with champagne. The goal is to throw ping-pong balls into the cups. Your opponent must drink the champagne in the cups your ping-pong balls land in. The first person who makes their opponent drink all of their cups wins. For those of you more seasoned gamers, it is exactly like beer pong but with champagne—a delightful game that gets you very drunk very fast.

Though staying in a fraternity dorm seems less than desirable, I enjoyed my time with Nico. He was absolutely the sweetest, most considerate and caring guy. I remember having a particularly rough week, and I was barely sleeping. I pulled yet another all-nighter, knowing I had to get up the next morning to work even harder. Nico, charmer that he was, had his younger fraternity brothers wake me up with a serenade and pancake breakfast in bed. He was the type of guy every woman should have the privilege of dating.

I had several Nico-like men throughout my twenties. I had the super-sweet guy who became more of a best friend. I am still friends with him and his family. I had the older gentlemen who treated me to four-course dinners and hundred-dollar bottles of wine. I had the hard-working, always-dedicated man who bought me gorgeous diamond jewelry. I have dated some beautiful and wonderful men . . . in my twenties.

So what happened in my thirties?

After my four-year relationship ended at the end of 2018, I started 2019 the same way I started my first year in Pensacola, on dating apps or at bars, saying yes to anyone who showed interest. I am in a phase in my life where most of my friends are seriously dating, engaged, married, or have been married at least once. If you remember, I have a true phobia of being alone, so I overcompensate by being the person everyone wants to date.

That person has poor discernment. I put myself in dangerous situations because of that. I've had to step back and identify who I am and what my values are, then ask myself if I'm sacrificing those values so I don't have to put in the work to truly discern who the right men are to have in my life. Therein lies the problem: I am quite aware of the reason, but how do I take action to move past it?

I am a romantic at heart. I read three different types of books at all times: (1) a professional book to elevate my career, (2) an autobiographical book to help elevate my personal life, and (3) a Nora Roberts or Jasmine Guillory romance novel to help me think about nothing and step away to my pretend life in romance world. I fantasize about being swept off my feet at the airport after a long week on the road or coming home to a bottle of wine and my favorite meal waiting for me, along with a foot rub and great sex. I fantasize about those things because in my twenties, though I wasn't traveling, I did have those romantic things in my life. But again, in my twenties, I set my standards to a level where the men in my life knew those expectations.

My parents taught me very early on that I am a queen and I should expect to be treated as such. Ultimately, what my parents wanted me to understand is I have far greater value than I allow myself to realize. I am generous to a fault at this stage of my life. I think it's because part of me feels guilty about being too scared to give of myself in my twenties because I was still dealing with the pain and hurt from my ex. In the chaos of my PTSD, when I lost the person I was before, I also lost my understanding of love.

In my work, it is so easy for me to connect to another leader or staff member and understand how to speak their language, meet them where they are, and walk them through the next steps in their journey through change. Applying that same understanding to my personal life is foreign. In my twenties, I preferred to be standoffish and not allow myself to be affected by the emotions and love men wanted to give me. In my thirties, I'm overcompensating for my inability to show emotion and love, and I blindly give of myself in a way that is not only unhealthy, it's dangerous.

So what do I do now? How do I live through this Season of Discernment, or, truly, this Season of *Lack* of Discernment? How do I move forward in a space that is uncomfortable and terrifying, and pushes me to be OK with my phobia of being alone? I don't have the answer for myself, much less you. What I can tell you is it's a work in progress. I find myself reaching out to my girlfriends more. I find myself mentally and emotionally stopping to pause, breathe, pray, and go to my safe space with God more, knowing that it may not bring answers, but it will bring me the peace I need to be OK with not being OK.

In this Season of Discernment, I am in the reality of growth, and it hurts. When I wrote this chapter, I purposely allowed myself to be alone. I had to allow the feelings and the reality to hit so I could connect to where my growth needed to be. I do not have it all together, and I do not understand why I am in this season. What I do know is there is something far greater for me than allowing myself to just live in moments of blind yeses. I am worth more than that man who verbally attacked me because I said something he didn't agree with. I am worth more than that man who didn't show up, much less call, when we were supposed to go out for dinner and drinks. And I am worth much more than any person who deigns to consider my time, my energy, or my efforts not valuable.

This Season of Discernment sucks, but it is teaching me that my worth will never be wrapped up in those who can't discern who I am and whose I am. I am totally and completely worth more.

And so are you.

SIXTEEN

Stress Doesn't Have to Own You

I was about twenty-two years old the first time my hair fell out in large chunks. I was in a season still fresh from the trauma of my PTSD diagnosis, and I was struggling with the darkness. I was having suicidal ideations at least a couple of times a week, my anxiety was causing me to severely grind my teeth, my bouts of rage were scaring even me, and my flashback night terrors and insomnia left me begging for just sixty minutes of sleep. To say I was stressed from the emotional and mental trauma I was going through is an understatement. Add on the fact that I was also barely making ends meet for myself, let alone my family, and you have a stress-induced-balding situation in the making.

It wasn't until 2019 that my current stylist and close friend identified that I actually had a disease called alopecia areata, which causes stress-induced extreme itching, dents in nails, or, in my case, loss of hair at the root, resulting in random bald spots. When I lost my hair at twenty-two, my stylist at the time and I decided to try to cover the hair loss with a much shorter haircut. My hair itself was damaged, so the shortened, mullet-like cut was less than appealing. My stylist did a phenomenal job, but she could only do so much with something she couldn't control.

When you realize your body's reaction to stress is to create bald patches in your head, you begin to rethink how you process stressors in your life.

When I was twenty-two, in addition to my own paycheck-to-paycheck existence, my parents and three siblings were living on my mother's and my paychecks. Growing up, both of my parents always worked, but as a professor, my father's paycheck was the larger of the two. Nonetheless, a family of six needs both paychecks to survive. During my senior year in high school, my family went through a huge financial transition. At the beginning of the year, my mother applied for and was promoted from a counseling position at a high school in another county to an assistant principal position at my school. The promotion came with a large salary increase and the joy of seeing my mother every day at school. My mother is my best friend, and all of my friends love her. She is like their super-honest mother who tells it like it is and encourages them to be themselves.

With this financial uptick, we had no qualms whatsoever about me applying to attend the only university that I wanted to go to, Wake Forest University. At the time, the annual tuition for Wake Forest was $50,000 per year, so the choice to apply was a bold one, knowing I could have applied to state schools whose tuition was easily half that amount. When I received the acceptance letter to Wake Forest in the fall of 2002, my parents and I agreed we would move forward with me attending Wake Forest in the fall of 2003 and mailed in the signed acceptance letter.

What transpired only a couple of months later is a book in and of itself. My father was put in a situation that was unfair and unjust, and it ultimately forced him to resign from his position in lieu of termination. At the same time, my mother was framed as the scapegoat for a teacher who violated testing policies. The superintendent decided anyone who had touched any of the tests would go down with the teacher. That included my mother, who was responsible for testing but had no control over a teacher stealing tests. The injustice was so blatant that it became a story on the local news, and at my high school graduation everyone booed the superintendent for his decision. Within the year, the superintendent mysteriously left to take a position in a school system on the West Coast. Interesting, no?

We quickly went from two substantial salaries to two zero salaries. Fortunately, my mother had a connection that got me my first job at the age of fourteen as a photographer's assistant, and I worked that job until graduating from high school. I also made money competing in pageants, which was typically set aside as scholarship money, and if the check wasn't made out directly to the university, it was made out directly to the pageant winner. The money from my work and pageants served as a source of income during the last half of my senior year and for over a decade later.

While my mother took another job opportunity as an assistant principal at a school in a different county within a few months, my father never went back to his role as a professor. It took him a couple of years to start working again, and seventeen years to find his fit. Although my mother's new job offered a consistent paycheck, it was nowhere near the money we needed to sustain a family of six, especially with one child—me—going off to college. My mom worked days as an assistant principal and nights as a sales associate for a department store in the mall.

By the time I finished high school, I was a certified nursing assistant and worked full-time for a home-healthcare agency during the summer, winter, and whenever I came home. My mother and I were the sole breadwinners for the family, and because the timing of when I started at Wake Forest coincided with the year my parents were actually making money, my financial aid was significantly less than we had anticipated. To go to the school of my dreams, I took out loans and worked part-time in a work-study program all four years of undergraduate study.

My family filed for bankruptcy during my junior year at Wake Forest, and we lost our house and one of our cars before the year was over. During my senior year, I realized I would graduate with over $50,000 of student loan debt, and I was working four jobs to help make ends meet for my family. Add in the continuous process of all four siblings beginning college, and it's no mystery why, at twenty-two years old, the stress of life was resulting in bald patches on my head.

I was bitter and constantly on edge. Living paycheck to paycheck is one thing, but knowing that paycheck may not make it to your bank account because your family needs it more is stressful and terrifying. I was stressed, angry, and confused. While I knew God was taking care of us, I couldn't understand why my dad wasn't. And although I am happy my dad finally found his fit, it was a seventeen-year process of my mom and me just doing what we could to keep the home together.

Finding your fit doesn't mean you abandon your family's needs. My dad eventually started a personal training business, which, to be honest, he was actually very good at, but it was never his true fit. Instead of pushing to make it a lucrative business, it became more of a side hustle—without an actual hustle to back up said side hustle. What I will never deny, though, is no matter what money my dad brought in, it all went directly to the family. He didn't take any of the money for himself; instead, he directly invested it into our needs.

I warred with a lot of emotions during that time, which compounded my stress. Though we lost our home, we lived in a decent rental home, we still had at least one working vehicle, and we were never in a position where living on the streets or living without some type of food was an option. We were struggling, but we were blessed.

When I left for Wake Forest at eighteen, I never went back to living at home. I love my family, and I love my parents, but the stress of caring for everyone and living there was not worth it. I visited often, but I enjoyed having an alternate universe where, for a few brief hours, my focus was only on me. I knew I couldn't survive on stress alone, and I needed balance. Finding that balance was difficult, and I soon found an unhealthy means of stress relief. It wasn't alcohol (I probably drink more now as a grown adult than I did in my twenties—it's amazing how quickly you can go through a bottle of wine when you're writing a book!). It wasn't prescribed medication or illegal drugs. I wasn't into drowning myself in substances that took away my self-control. What I did was start masking my feelings through relationships or casual sex.

I fully believe everyone's sexuality is their own decision, but I also don't believe in using anything or anyone, including sex, as a way to keep from dealing with your real emotions and issues. If I wasn't in a relationship, I was with a man who enjoyed caring for me. I enjoyed the casual relationships significantly more than the serious ones. There were no strings and no expectations. It was a temporary stress relief, but truthfully, having an outlet that required no work from me besides just saying yes to consensual and safe sex . . . well, it brought me happiness.

Happiness is sadly fleeting, and I soon found myself even more stressed. It was hard for me to balance the needs of my family; the adult world of work, bills, and just trying to survive; and my personal life, which may have been brimming with men, but they were mostly men who were there one day and gone the next. Instead of finding balance, I was plugging the holes stress was causing in my life with one activity or person after another.

I easily had two or three breakdowns per month, sometimes around other people and sometimes alone. I was not OK, and I knew I needed to find some way to achieve healthy balance. It would take me years to actually reach out for help, but in my late twenties I started going back to counseling. I couldn't really handle my problems if I didn't enlist the right help to consistently cope with them. I coupled the counseling with a guided meditative service offered by the hospital I was working at then, which instilled a foundation for breathing through the pressure and stress of life. The counseling and meditative services didn't solve everything, but these resources provided balance and coping tools, helping me understand that I didn't have to just sit and live in the stress and anger of my life.

By the time I moved to Pensacola, my siblings were able to provide for and help out my family, so the pressure was starting to subside. With the success of my brother Julius's baseball career, and my dad serving as his primary trainer, my dad's personal training business was becoming more lucrative. By 2019, my mother had been promoted to a school principal and spent several successful years in that role, and all the kids were grown and out of the house. My parents were finally able to rebuild their lives and their home with minimal help from us kids.

While the pressures of my family life had steadily subsided, I knew I was still putting added pressure on my personal life. I still wasn't fully investing in balancing out how I allowed the right people into my life. I found myself in a situation with a man who proved to be very dangerous. The short but volatile relationship triggered my PTSD, and I spent about six weeks having flashback nightmares and reliving the trauma from my ex. Four weeks into the relationship, I went in for an appointment with my stylist, and we found my stress-induced alopecia areata had resurfaced, and I had a patch of hair missing on a very visible spot on the side of my head. While we were able to hide the patch, I knew it was time to move on from the stress of allowing yet another person into my life who didn't deserve my time.

Coping and balancing are a constant struggle for me, as I'm sure they are for many of you. It's hard to remind yourself to handle stress appropriately when you're in the middle of it. What I continue to learn and teach myself is that I don't have to let stress own my life. I have the ability to utilize all the tools around me and everything that I've learned in my life to acknowledge the stress, understand the emotions around it, and identify how I need to move forward in a direction that doesn't compound the stress but helps me healthily work through it.

We can't always control the stressors in our life, but we can build a foundation of strength that will help us handle any stressors that come our way. Working through stress takes time and grace. Know that you will never work through anything all at once. It takes years of consistently not allowing yourself to be completely fueled and owned by the stress to begin to find the healthy coping tools to find the balance you need to proactively own your response to stressful situations.

Healthy coping tools look different for everyone, so I challenge you to find three key tools that you can use when you feel stress mounting.

Maybe it's steady, meditative breathing. There are plenty of free apps that will support your meditation journey, and trust me, the breathing alone makes a world of difference in reducing stress.

It could be a walk, run, or workout to help physically release the impact of stress on your body. I found that I feel more vulnerable to the negative effects of stress when I haven't been working out consistently. My regular workouts may look different than yours, so identify what gives you that physical release.

Or it could be something artistic, like writing, drawing, musical expression, or creating artwork.

Whatever it is, think through what consistently brings you peace and use that as your coping tool. We all deserve the balance of not letting stress own us. We just have to put in the effort to take back that control and own our response to the stressors in our life.

SEVENTEEN

Your Crew

Do you remember watching dance movies, like *Step Up*, *Step Up 2 the Streets*, or *You Got Served*? Aside from the original *Step Up*, showcasing the beauty that is Channing Tatum, and *You Got Served*, showing yet again the amazing talent of Marques Houston (yes, I'm a sucker for movies with gorgeous men who can dance!), the premise of the movies is the importance of having a crew.

These movies chronicle the lives of underdog hip-hop dancers who gear up to compete in a dance competition or showcase. Throughout the movie, you watch the main characters struggle with their crew, and the crew endures an identity crisis. Inevitably, the crew almost breaks up, then they come back together as a family. The strength of the crew empowers them to take over the enemy (another dance crew) and show that they could only be victorious as a family.

Though flashy dance moves, shirtless men (who always manage to have impeccable six-packs), and catchy music draw you in, the concept that you leave the theater understanding is that a crew isn't necessarily the family you're born into but the family you choose.

Growing up in a family of six, my parents were always quick to remind me that my siblings were my perpetual crew. Like most kids with younger siblings, I went through a phase where I was less than pleased with my parent-imposed crew.

There was one time when I was about five years old, and my brother Lou was having one of his many too-much-energy-in-public moments. He was yet again running through the department store where Mom was shopping. He loved hiding in the middle of the circular racks of clothing and jumping out at innocent bystanders, terrifying them. My mother had barely reached thirty at this time, and I reflect now and think, *Wow, she had the patience of a saint!* During Lou's energized moments, she would quickly gather us up, find an area with chairs or a couch, and put me in charge of Lou patrol.

I hated Lou patrol. Lou was born full of energy, adventure, and rebellion. I was born shy, socially introverted, and very obedient. Lou patrol always meant being thrust in an uncomfortable situation where I had to talk to strangers and apologize for Lou jumping out and scaring them or asking them hundreds of questions. Lou was only the beginning of my sibling crew, but he was enough. While I loved him dearly, at five years old, I was desperately considering seeking applicants to start a new crew.

Once Julius and Faythe joined the scene, the Tobias Siblings Crew was born with me as the unfortunate and typically unwilling leader. Flash forward to 2019, and I cannot imagine my life without my familial crew. My siblings, Lou especially, have been my rocks. During times of grief, turmoil, and trauma, they have not only stuck by my side but dared anyone to try to mess with me. The great thing about the Tobias Siblings Crew is that nobody would dare mess with us. With one, there is strength; with four, there is insurmountable power.

While I did not choose this crew, I can't imagine not having this crew in my life. The fierce pride, comfort in being your authentic self, and protectiveness you feel with a group of people are just a few of the criteria for a healthy crew.

There is such a thing as an unhealthy crew. In an unhealthy crew, you find yourself questioning your value. You may feel as if you don't belong and be scared to leave the room because of the ever-present sense that someone is talking about you. That is the criteria for a nonsupportive, unhealthy, get-out-of-there-right-now crew.

After graduating from Wake Forest, I stayed in Winston-Salem, the university's home base. A handful of my friends at Wake Forest stayed in the city, too, but most of them dispersed to their hometowns or to new towns for their next career moves. My girlfriends who stayed were also part of another preexisting crew, my sorority.

During my time at Wake Forest, a crew of five of us was formed, with three of us also being part of my sorority crew, but all of us cementing our friendship bond from our time at university. To this day, we still have a group text and make a point of inviting each other to special events in our lives. We also update each other throughout the year on big events and continue to support and love each other as if we were still in college. One of these crew members is such a deep and invested crew member that our parents joke that we are twins. In college, people always thought we were twins, but as we became older, our bond grew to a point where our connection merged into the type of bond that I can only hope twins share.

While being in a sorority technically allocates a crew of lifelong sisters to you, my actual chosen, these-are-my-girls crew was limited to those women whom I could truly share my life with. Our friendship was forged from joining the same sorority, but it remains because of our endless bond of love and authentic and honest connection. About a year postgraduation, though, these girlfriends moved out of state, while I still remained.

I had an on-again, off-again relationship with a guy who would eventually become more of a best friend than a boyfriend. He accompanied me to my senior prom, and he is still someone I respect and love dearly. Since my Wake Forest female crew was no longer in existence, my boyfriend introduced me to his guy friends. I spent the next several months just hanging with the boys, until finally one of the guys said that he thought I would get along with his girlfriend and her friends.

A couple of nights later, we were all hanging out at my boyfriend's friend's house. That night, I met his girlfriend, whom I will call Sasha, and her best friend. At first, I was a little scared of Sasha. She had all the energy of a young Lou. As someone who is secretly shy, that terrified me, and all I could think was, *No! Lou 2.0!* Her best friend, though, was a calmer spirit whom I felt an instant connection with. After spending a few hours with them, I realized they were women just like me—recent college graduates just trying to figure out how to navigate this messy world and decide what to do next.

They instantly took me under their wings and introduced me to their group of girlfriends. I will be forever grateful to them for their compassion and openness. To this day, these women are still part of my crew. Every year, a group of seven of us take a trip to a new destination. Our most recent trip took us to Lake Tahoe, California.

While I have now been friends with these women for about a decade, among the group there are friendships that have spanned twenty to thirty years. It's beautiful and intimidating to be part of a crew with that much history. With decades of friendship come decades of bonds that are hard to break into, but though their bonds are strong, they are not closed and by no means limited. The bonds they have just make them that much more protective of the friends who are part of our crew.

During our Tahoe trip, I felt as though I finally allowed myself to trust and be a little more vulnerable with these women. Vulnerability is hard for me, especially in a crew of people I admire. These women include four mothers, two mothers of twins and one mother of five, and all seven of us have worked or are currently working in the professional industry. To say we are a force to be reckoned with is an understatement.

As part of this crew, we have made it important to not just gloss over the hard stuff going on in our lives. To begin our Tahoe trip, we decided to fly to and meet up in San Francisco, then drive the three and a half hours to Tahoe. During the drive, we each shared life updates. These updates opened us up to pure, raw vulnerability. We discussed the difficulties of married life and family life, the vulnerability of past traumas and how they were affecting us now, and our satisfaction or dissatisfaction with our professional lives. We just talked and allowed that open space to be available for whomever needed it. This, my friends, is what I call a crew. Though I may feel insecure sometimes around women who have such a long history, we invited each other into this crew. That invitation includes authenticity, vulnerability, and, yes, sometimes a little discomfort, but the kind of discomfort that pushes us all closer together.

When Sasha introduced me to her girlfriends, that also included friends of her girlfriends who had shorter-term relationships but were still connected. One of those friends introduced me to a much larger crew of about sixty people that did not include the girlfriends I visited Tahoe with. This larger crew was comprised of men and women; some in relationships, some single, but all shared the common bond of living in Winston-Salem.

In addition to the crew I visited Tahoe with, I also became part of this larger crew. I quickly learned the difference between a healthy and an unhealthy crew. While there were a lot of people within this crew who truly loved and appreciated each other, there were also a select few who were, shall we say, "mean girls," who made it a point to talk about other members of the crew behind their backs. I was at a stage in my life where I believed in authentic honesty no matter how painful it might be, but I was also still insecure about releasing any friends for fear that if I didn't have a lot of friends, I wouldn't have a lot of value in my life.

A couple of years into this crew, I started dating a new guy who was blunt, assertive, and a man with one of the biggest hearts. He adored me, cared for me, and fiercely protected me. He was not a fan of this crew. He constantly asked me how I could be friends with people who were so mean to each other, but I just blew it off.

A couple of years later, I hosted a Christmas party at my house with a mix of people present, including members from this not-so-kind crew. My mother, as usual, was present, and she helped shine a light on the reality of this not-so-kind crew.

Note that my mother is not only a member of my crew, she is my ultimate "check yourself" crew. I have a handful of people who are part of this crew. The difference between a regular crew and a "check yourself" crew is that these people have an ability to tell you the hard truths that not everyone has the ability or tact to do. The "check yourself" crew are who you go to because they have an investment in you as a person and are able to objectively provide the feedback you need to consider, especially when you're making questionable decisions in your life.

My mother served as a necessary "check yourself" crew member during my Christmas party. There, some of my not-so-kind-crew members were continuously talking about each other when one person would leave the room, or making snide, petty remarks about people not present at the party. My mother, in her infinite wisdom, looked at these crew members and said, "Why are you guys so mean?"

I was initially mortified, but then my mother turned to me and said, "How can you be friends with people who are so mean?" The palpable silence and the smug look on the rest of the attendees' faces that read, "Thank you so much for saying that," put me in my place. Shortly after that night, a falling-out occurred with that crew, and I never returned to that group. During the falling-out, I remember angrily cutting them down for always talking about each other and never saying anything to anyone's face. Great idea in theory; not such a great idea when you provoke these now-unhappy crew members to tell you what they really think about you. It was heated and nasty, and although at first I was upset and sad to lose these friends, my boyfriend and my mother affirmed this was not only the right thing to do but the healthy thing to do.

While I have not reconnected in person with most of the members of that crew, with time, maturity and social media, we have all maintained at least a virtual connection.

It is important to remember that there is a need to have a crew outside of just your immediate family that you see every day. This crew could be one person you connect with or six, but this crew is important because they are part of your healing journey. When we give ourselves a chance to look outside of our immediate circle, we also open ourselves up to a kind of growth that is only possible through a perspective outside of our own.

So, who is your crew? If this is the first time you've ever thought about a crew, I encourage you to think about the people or person in your life who brings you the comfort and peace you need to be your authentic self—the person or people you can reach out to and just talk.

If this seems daunting, start small. Maybe even reach out virtually to someone through Messenger or text message. The message could just be a simple "Hey, I was thinking about you and thought I would see how you're doing."

The first rule about being part of a crew is to be a supportive crew member. Just as you want your crew to support you, you also must support your crew. Start off by offering support or a kind word, and allow your crew to slowly blossom into a supportive, encouraging, authentic, and honest relationship.

You have the chance to build your own crew, a crew that will help support your journey through growth, healing, purpose, and fulfillment. Be selective, be purposeful, and most of all be authentic in whom you choose to be part of your crew.

EIGHTEEN

But Do You Actually Need a Glass of Wine?

Let's be honest: I really enjoy wine. I know I've alluded to my love of wine, so I might as well come clean: I've made a point of learning about and embedding myself in the wine culture. When I lived in North Carolina, I spent two or three times a week at a wine bar or vineyard owned by a good friend; I visited Napa Valley with a girlfriend, where we took an all-day bus excursion to four different wineries; I have seen the documentary *Somm*, about the journey to becoming a master sommelier, at least ten times; and after several work visits to Oregon, I became a wine club member at Willamette Valley Vineyards, in Turner, Oregon. (I have no regrets about this membership, to be clear.)

With my love and passion for wine culture, it should come as no surprise that I also made a trip to France to explore my wine passion even more.

In the early spring of 2016, a dear friend, whom we shall call Vivi, invited me on a river cruise through Bordeaux, France. The vineyard she was working at was hosting a celebratory ten- day trip for their wine club members, and the head vintner would join, providing excellent tips and tricks of the wine world. The cruise would set sail in the late fall of that same year, and the cost for the trip was discounted and included every-thing except for personal excursions, even an onboard ship credit to buy fancy souvenirs at the ship's boutique.

After taking a couple of days to think it through, I agreed to join Vivi on the trip. To be honest, I didn't even need the couple of days, but as a "responsible adult," I thought I should at least pretend to think it through.

After saying yes to the trip, I paid for everything—one year later, al-most to the day, I would suffer my thirty-thousand-dollar pay cut. Talk about divine timing!

The trip was a wine lover's dream. Once we landed in France, we grabbed much needed French coffee at the French version of Starbucks, gathered our fellow cruise friends, and took a bus to our ship.

For those of you who have only been on oceanic cruises, and while I do recommend any cruise, the river cruise ship was superior, in my es-timation, because it held a maximum of a hundred passengers. It was small, beautiful, and intimate, and within the first two days, Vivi and I made friends with most of the staff on the ship.

A typical day for us included a sunrise wake-up to work out in the ship's gym overlooking the water, an excursion through whatever French city our ship docked in, lunch in the city, some historical sightseeing, then dinner and music back on the ship. We were both fresh from compet-ing in bodybuilding contests, so we were still in the habit of early-morn-ing workouts. Our workouts coincided with when the cruise ship staff came on duty, and they walked through the gym to go outside for smoke breaks or to reach other areas of the ship. It's no wonder we made friends with the staff, as we were the only other people awake when they started their shifts.

We biked through the French countryside, visited countless châ-teaus, spent time at the prestigious Rémy Martin cognac facility, and ac-tually ran through a French vineyard in a rainstorm. We would always depart at sunset, combining a beautiful view with a lovely glass of wine. Every time we made it back onto the cruise ship, the staff had our favorite glass of wine ready for us, and at dinner, we had a four-course French meal with a wine pairing for each course.

Vivi and I made a pact that, no matter what, we were going to enjoy every aspect of this trip and make a point to ensure every single person also enjoyed themselves. We befriended every passenger and every staff member on the ship. When I befriended the onboard musician, our conversation escalated into me singing "Put Your Records On" by Corinne Bailey Rae and "Rehab" by the late Amy Winehouse for the entire cruise ship. Vivi and I even provided an impromptu version of Coolio's "Gangsta's Paradise" because, why not?

When we finally returned to the States, I found myself confused when I came home and a glass of wine, a robe, and fancy toiletries weren't waiting on my bed. The experience was phenomenal and further spurred my delight for the beauty that is wine.

While I love and appreciate the culture of wine, I also have a tendency to use it as an easy escape tool when life gets a little rough. Have you ever used the phrase "I need a glass of wine," or my favorite, "Just leave the bottle"? While I am joking (a little!), it is important to understand the difference between enjoying a beverage and self-medicating.

Self-medicating can be described as using a substance—for me, wine—to help soothe yourself when you get worried, anxious, frustrated, angry, or any other emotion that makes it difficult for you to handle your situation. The difference between self-medicating and "just having a drink" is that the substance you choose becomes a consistent go-to tool to cover up the situation you are dealing with. It never really takes away the situation; it just blinds you for a short period of time. When I am ready to self-medicate instead of deal with my problems, my mind tends to go through the following thought processes:

It's been a bad day. Break out the wine!

It's been a day of biting my tongue so I don't tell people how I really feel. Two glasses, please.

It's been a day full of not feeling valued. Where's the bottle?

Or my all-time favorite: *There were screaming or crying children involved in my day. I need multiple bottles of wine!*

I found myself shifting from just having a glass of wine with dinner or to close out my day to drinking wine to help mitigate the stressful activities of my day. I was no longer drinking to enjoy but as an unhealthy coping tool. For example, I recently noticed that when I was dating someone I knew I really needed to end things with, instead of facing the reality of the situation, I would typically drink a glass or two of wine before seeing him, so I could ease the pressure. I told myself I was just reducing my anxiety, since dating new people can be stressful, although that's what my physician-prescribed anxiety medication is technically for. What I was really doing was trying to forget that I needed to take uncomfortable action in a situation where the result would be me being alone yet again.

I can't operate that way and expect to actually work through my problems, and neither can you.

So what should you do when you find yourself in a situation where self-medication seems like the best temporary solution to your current problem? Try asking yourself this question: "Will self-medicating help me realistically work through my problem?" Allow yourself the space to answer the question first. This technique does not work if you ask the question while drinking a glass of wine. Trust me, I've tried.

When you are honest with yourself about the purpose for your self-medicating activity, you also have to be honest about the root cause of needing something to ease the pressure, anxiety, or fear.

The more we allow things to keep us from handling real emotions and real life, the more power we give to things that don't deserve that power. While you may not have an immediate solution for how to handle the constant barrage of emotions and fears that may surround you, giving yourself a chance to think through what you actually need as a long-term coping tool will allow you to take ownership of finding an appropriate solution instead of depending on something else to be the solution for you.

This is where the coping tools and techniques we discussed previously come into play. This is your opportunity to own a permanent solution to a problem instead of a temporary Band-Aid.

So how does this relate back to the statement "I need a glass of wine"? Instead of using your situation or frustration as the reason to have a glass of wine or to self-medicate, separate the purpose for your glass of wine or other activity that you use for self-medicating. Instead of it serving as an unhealthy Band-Aid, reset it to serve as a celebratory act.

You should never "need" something to bring you fulfillment, but you can have something that represents your ability to own your life and own your journey. You can have a glass of wine just because you want a delicious Cabernet Sauvignon to share with your even more delicious pizza, or because it's a beautiful, warm spring day and you want a crisp Pinot Grigio to complement the day.

Think about where your self-medicating needs to be amended to actually using the coping skills and tools you have available to manage your emotions. Bring back the rewards and celebrations in your life by focusing on your own long-term healing.

NINETEEN

Surviving and Building Your Empire

Back in my twenties, when I lived paycheck to paycheck, I remember dreading checking my bank account. This was before cell phones had an app for your bank, so you had to go online, go to the bank website, remember your username and password (or reset it for the hundredth time, like I usually did), then log in to your account. Without fail, my bank account revealed what I already knew: I had what could be rounded up to zero dollars.

You always know it's bad when you can feel the bright red, flashing negative account balance before you even see it.

While I would love to tell you this was a rare occurrence, it was not. I stayed in and out of negative balance for the larger part of my early and mid-twenties. On top of that, I also had horrible credit, which resulted from two events: One was a medical bill from when my car steered itself into a ditch a couple of months after I graduated from Wake Forest. I never received the medical bill because it went to the wrong address, so I was considered in default before I even knew I had to pay any money. The second event was stolen identity. Somebody decided to have gastroenterology surgery and go on a shopping spree, all under my name, racking up lots of debt they never paid for.

My credit score was abysmal, maybe a hundred points over the minimum score. I learned all of this when my parents came with me to try to buy a new car to replace my totaled one, only to find out my poor credit score would increase my annual percentage rate on the new car to double digits, and the credit bureaus did not think I was responsible enough to own it alone, so I needed one of my parents to cosign. While my parents' credit was better than mine, their score was still poor from the bankruptcy, student debt that they both had accrued, and their own credit mishaps.

A friend suggested I reach out to her financial counselor to get some advice on how to not suck at finances. The counselor recommended I first focus on fixing my credit score. She suggested I get a low-interest credit card, spend money I would usually put on my debit card on my credit card, then pay it off each month. I know what you're thinking: *Twenty-something with a credit card—oh, this will be good!* Believe me when I say I was very focused on following the financial counselor's advice. For almost a decade, I didn't use that credit card for anything other than purchases I was already planning on making, and then I immediately paid them off.

When you make no money and you desperately just want enough money to feel secure, you do what you can to build that security. When I finally started working for the hospital I was at prior to moving into consulting, I saw a ten-thousand-dollar increase in my salary, and I was finally starting to see the light at the end of the negative-bank-account tunnel. I started actually putting money into my savings account, building up my credit, and, dare I say, making smart adult purchasing decisions.

When I transitioned from the hospital to consulting, I had a few thousand dollars saved up in the bank, another ten-thousand-dollar increase in salary, and a steadily rising credit score. At the end of 2014, my first year in Pensacola, I decided to buy a house. Realizing the cost of living was incredibly affordable and the market was fairly hot, it seemed like the right time. By March of 2015, I was the owner of an adorable three-bedroom, two-bath house, with an affordable, some might even say cheap, mortgage. At the beginning of that year, when I was promoted to a full-time consulting role, I had also received a twenty-thousand-dollar pay increase, but my mother advised me to buy my house based on my previous salary and live on my previous salary, so I did . . . until I didn't.

Within that same year, I received another twenty-thousand-dollar pay increase due to my successful results with my consulting clients. I also started dating the man I would spend four years of my life with. At the time, he had a job that didn't match my salary, but it did provide a paycheck. When he moved in at the end of 2015, I didn't think much about our finances. All I expected was that we would now split the bills, which also helped contribute to my savings account.

By the beginning of 2016, I had more than doubled my salary from 2014 and my credit was considered very good. So I celebrated by buying a new car on my current salary, not my previous salary. I thought I deserved a little treat! While I was not wrong to reward myself, I didn't adjust my spending to compensate for the new car payment. The car was considered a luxury car, and I named her Laila Ali—yes, after Muhammad Ali's daughter. She definitely floats like a butterfly and stings like a bee, and I have never regretted this purchase.

What I did regret was not sustaining my healthy financial mind-set. As a kid, my parents always joked that I was the first person to give away all my money to the church or to someone in need instead of keeping it for myself. While that generosity never went away, I needed the financial discipline in my twenties to know how to save my money and use it wisely so I would have the funds to support that generosity.

Generosity and supporting those in need does not necessarily mean those you are in a relationship with. When you're in a relationship, you tend to think with your feelings and not your mind. I cannot blame any of my financial decisions on my ex. I have responsibility for them, but when you're dating you tend to go out a little more, drink a little more, and splurge a little more. I started putting more on my credit card and paying off less. I was now up to two personal credit cards. One was technically allocated for business, and one was supposed to be personal, but the line between business and personal was often blurry.

We went on trips abroad almost every year, which we both started off funding, until he lost his job. The trips from 2016 moving forward were largely funded by me, even after my thirty-thousand-dollar pay cut. Our expenses were piling up at an alarming rate, so I found myself shifting to using my credit cards more, my debit card less, and not making the necessary payments to move myself out of debt. My debt skyrocketed, and I was easily close to $100,000 in debt from student loans and credit cards.

One smart thing that I did in 2016 was connect with a dear friend and sorority sister who was a financial counselor. She was a godsend. I knew nothing about investing, but she guided me toward squirreling away a large chunk of money and splitting it between stand-alone investment accounts connected to additional life insurance and long-term-disability accounts. She also had me deposit money into a separate savings account that I could not touch without contacting her. She helped me set a budget to guide my spending, but in 2017, when I took the large pay cut, instead of going back to her for support and to reset my budget, I foolishly tried to figure it out on my own.

I was drowning in debt, and I knew I was hitting the point of no return when I saw something in my bank account I had not seen since my twenties: a zero balance. By 2018, I had depleted my checking account and most of the thousands of dollars in my savings account and was yet again living paycheck to paycheck. How in the hell did this happen with the kind of money I was making? Easy. I may have been making money, but I was not paying attention to the money coming in and the money going out.

I had added my ex onto my checking account earlier the year before, and while for some people a shared checking account is a great idea, for me it was a way of supporting him without having to pay attention to what that support looked like. While, yes, I allowed him to use whatever money he wanted, at the end of the day, I enabled the egregious spending of money. Though I was making $30,000 less than my maximum salary, I was still making a really good paycheck and was in denial of how much money I was actually spending.

When we finally broke up at the end of 2018, I reached out to my financial counselor to ask for her help in resetting my financial life. We refocused my mind-set beyond just surviving and back to building the empire I had started building with my savings accounts, investment accounts, and smart adult spending. We realigned my finances with my actual minus-$30,000 salary and set a plan for how to pay off my debts. When I received my promotion and pay increase about four months later, we sat down again to look at how to shift my additional finances to more savings and investment so I wouldn't make the same mistakes as in the past.

For me, 2019 is quite literally the year of surviving and building my new empire. While I had built my original financial successes on good advice, the foundation was unstable. When I had no money, it was much easier for me to save to survive. When I had money, I started spending my empire before I ever built it. I gave generously to all of my vices—relationships, shopping, fun—anything and everything that allowed me to feel successful. Success is built on a strong foundation of hard work, dedication, and discipline. Does that mean you can't splurge every now and then? Absolutely not, but for me, I needed to be mindful of the difference between splurging and blindly spending because I had it to spend. Just because you have it to spend now does not mean it will always be there.

I continue to learn from the repercussions of my frivolous annihilation of my previous empire, but with this new empire, I am building my foundation on rock instead of sand.

I encourage you to think about the empire you are building. Do you find yourself constantly fluctuating between a state of stressful spending and frugal savings? Where are the balance and strength in the foundation of your empire based?

While I fully support enjoying life, I also fully support taking pride in the empire you are building for yourself and for those who are learning from you. Build your empire on a sustainable foundation. Begin budgeting and setting good spending behaviors now, no matter how old you are. It is never too late. It is your empire and your responsibility, so build it, strengthen it, and never let anyone or anything knock it down.

TWENTY

Thriving and Leaving Nothing Behind

Something precious happens when we start to think about our own mortality: we stop thinking about the "what ifs" and start thinking about the "what now."

Recently, a dear friend of mine, let's call her Violet, was faced with her own mortality when she was diagnosed with stage IV cancer. She found out a few weeks after we went on a work trip together. Violet had told me she was having some back pain that she was planning on getting checked out by a doctor in the coming weeks. What was supposed to be a checkup maybe leading to a prescription for muscle relaxants turned into an eye-opening and jaw-dropping conversation about the next steps in dealing with stage IV cancer.

Violet endured months of chemotherapy and radiation treatment until she and her husband decided her quality of life was more important than enduring more treatments to lessen the impact of cancer. Violet has over twenty years on me. She has lived a fulfilled and amazing life, and she and her husband were ready to just enjoy the time they still had. They made the decision to transition from the hospital to home hospice care.

Violet is one of those people who radiates life. She is known throughout our company for her phenomenal client results, amazing relationship-building skills, and keen wit. When we first met, it was the beginning of 2015, and I was shadowing her on one of my first consulting visits. We met in the hotel lobby for dinner. Violet knew every waiter and bartender by name, and they knew her by name. When she ordered a martini, I, of course, ordered one, too. When the bartender brought our martinis, I swear the glass was bigger than my head. Within twenty minutes, Violet had finished martini number one and was on to martini number two, unfazed. I had barely touched martini number one, and the pure magnitude of it was giving me a buzz.

We spent that night getting to know each other, honestly and transparently. I was amazed at how open she was about everything. I admired her ability to unabashedly give of herself in a way that invited whomever she was talking with to feel connected and engaged with every aspect of her life. I have no shame in saying that I started utilizing that innate skill of hers in all of my interactions at work and in my personal life.

Violet taught me how to connect with clients first and build trust and a relationship before ever trying to consult with them. She taught me how to effortlessly guide clients in the direction that leads to them discovering their own "aha" moments instead of me taking credit for something new I was teaching them. She showed me that every person you encounter has a story that deserves to be heard, acknowledged, and respected, and that it's important to take the time to invest in people.

When I was with Violet, I laughed so hard my stomach hurt, I opened myself up to discussing parts of my life that I never revealed to anyone else, and I soaked in every bit of wisdom she imparted. She was and still is my mentor, my friend, and my confidante.

When Violet was diagnosed with cancer, she shared the news with the president of our side of the company, who then relayed the news to the rest of us. It hit each and every one of us like a rock. Cancer doesn't discriminate, but of all the people I know, Violet was the one person I was certain would outlive me. My heart broke in two when I got the news about her diagnosis. I was in the middle of a meeting with my coworkers, and I couldn't stop the tears from falling down my face.

I am not a crier. It takes an act of God or stubbing my pinky toe for me to cry. When I was five years old, I remember being at my mom's father's funeral. Everyone was blubbering, and the sorrow and grief were palpable. As a little girl, my grandfather was my best friend. Originally from Cuba, he had met my grandmother in Jamaica. To me, he always smelled like Cuban cigars and happiness. My mother swears he never smoked cigars (this is an endless debate with us), but I remember that thick cigar smell at five years old. His death was one of the first deaths I experienced. Two years prior, my father's mother passed away. I was too young to understand what was going on, but I still remember the raw emotions. What I remember from both funerals was the admonition from the elders to stop crying. Crying wasn't celebrating their life but just bringing more sorrow.

I took that admonition with me into adulthood, and I always find it hard to cry without thinking about the strong resolve my parents showed at the funerals of their respective parents. What is important to remember is, regardless of those ingrained habits or even questionable examples we have seen from our childhood about how to grieve or how to express emotions, we each still have our own unique way of expressing our feelings.

In the situation with Violet, I allowed the feelings to come in the middle of a professional environment surrounded by people who have said more than once, "We love your energy and positivity." At that particular time, I didn't think about what they thought about me, and I didn't think about how my expression of emotion would impact my work. All I thought was that my friend who has breathed life into me since we met could be closer to taking her last breath than I realized.

I spent easily ten minutes locked in the bathroom stall, having a full-on cry session. When I returned to the office space, my coworkers looked at me and asked what had happened, and instead of blowing it off so I didn't seem vulnerable, I told them the painful truth. I said, "A woman whom I have considered a dear friend and mentor and who is also one of our colleagues was diagnosed with stage IV cancer. The prognosis has hit our side of the company hard, and we are all just trying to figure out our feelings while loving on her." The response from my coworkers was simple: they showed me unconditional grace, love, and respect and let me know they were there for whatever I needed.

I'm just going to put this out there: physical death is inevitable. For me, my faith guides me to know that my soul has an eternal place in heaven even though my body will fail. Violet also shares my faith, and throughout her journey with cancer she has shone her light and her faith even brighter. She started a blog where she provides almost daily testimonials. Violet has always been tactfully honest. Her ability to share the difficult moments with positivity astounds me and pushes me to remember that our lives are the only ones we have to live. It's empowering to watch someone else's journey and to live it alongside them.

Violet embodies the idea of thriving and leaving nothing behind. She and her husband have been living out this phase of her life openly and vulnerably. While I am not there to see the hard parts, the struggles and the difficult decisions they had to make to forgo treatment to have a better quality of the rest of this life, I am there to read her blogs and text her my love and talk with her about how much her life has inspired me. When I asked her if she minded if I wrote this chapter inspired by her, her exact words were, "I am honored." *She's* honored? I'm honored to have a friend so gracious to let me share part of her life in a book about being fearless.

Being fearless doesn't mean you have no fear; it means you don't allow that fear to control you. What I learned from Violet is simple: fear has no place in a life where we were meant to thrive. When I was in my dark places, death seemed to be surrounding me. There was a time in my life early on after my diagnosis of PTSD that I didn't think I would make it to see my thirtieth year. I couldn't imagine dealing with the pain and the heartache that I was going through for much longer, and ending my life seemed like a much better option. I allowed the fear of living to control my ability to actually live.

When I look back on where I was during that time and where I am now, I think about the hard work, the pain, the suffering, and the never-ending journey toward living my life, with all of its imperfections, with all of its ups and downs, and sideways and upside downs. I think about not allowing anything in this world to keep me from not just surviving but thriving.

This is your time to thrive. This is your time to embrace this perfectly imperfect life. Be the fearlessly made person you were always meant to be. Live this life with all of its setbacks, heartaches, joyfulness, and laughter in a way that only you can.

You are the owner of your one life.

Be light.

Be strength.

Be fearless.

Be you.

Acknowledgments

Writing a book is hard! Nobody tells you that when you write a book you have to actually think about the words you want to say! I would like to take this time to thank all of the wine that has sustained me through this process. Just kidding!

When I think about whom to thank, I think about the people in my life who surround me with love, support, and honesty. I have not always been driven to share the stories that are included in this book. But I was encouraged and inspired by the amazing people around me. We all have a story to tell. Some of our stories look similar, some of them look vastly different, but at the end of the day our stories deserve to be shared. I was reminded that I have the ability to be the voice for those who will never feel comfortable using their own voice. To be that voice, I had to have my own inspirational voices challenging me to be authentic and honest in my own story.

My immediate family has instilled unconditional faith in God in my life. My parents, Drs. Tobias, always told me I could accomplish anything I set my mind to. They have pushed and challenged me to always do and be more. They have guided me to never settle for anything less than my best and to also be OK with the uncomfortable. They embody a faith-driven, imperfect life that is focused on thriving through each and every journey, and I am grateful that their guidance and determination have brought me to this point, where I could truthfully share such an important part of my life.

To the Tobias Siblings Crew: Each of you has had my back since you were born. Thank you for allowing your stories to be part of my story and for coming up with your own special code names, because life isn't fun without your endless senses of humor. The unconditional bond and the love we share are unbreakable. I am honored to be your big sister and blessed to always have you by my side. Thank you for literally fighting my battles. Thank you for never letting me move forward in this life alone. Thank you for being my confidantes, my role models, and my inspirations.

To my extended family on my mom's and dad's sides—my uncles, aunts, cousins, and fearless grandmother: Thank you each for your support and love. Thank you for always sending me messages of love and endless support. Thank you for always being proud of me and for never questioning the paths I've chosen. Thank you for the long and purposeful conversations about the role of God in my life, and thank you for never letting me lose focus on my faith and my purpose.

To my Pageant Family Crew: Thank you for your true and never-ending friendship. Thank you to my mentors who believed in the power of my voice and in breaking down barriers. Thank you for not allowing antiquated societal viewpoints to keep you from pushing and supporting me to be the top of my field. To my pageant "sistas": We will always be enough, and I am grateful to have shared this journey with you. To all of my other pageant ladies: You have been my shining stars and my inspiration. Your resilience, endless mentorship, and camaraderie drove me to never doubt my abilities. Thank you for your stories, your strength, and your love.

To my North Carolina Crew: Each of you represents so many purposeful parts of my life. From my days in middle school and high school to my days after undergraduate, you all have remained an integral part of my life. From porch dinners to winery and wine bar meetups whenever I'm in town, I have always felt connected to each of you, no matter where I lived. There are annual girls' trips to new locations, long-distance phone dates, virtual wine dates, and the never-ending ability for us to pick up as if it has only been minutes instead of months or years since we've been together. Your love and support, your ability to help me feel enough just as I am, have strengthened me and brought me to this phase in my life. Thank you for sharing your stories with me and being so open to being part of my story.

To my sorority sisters: Thank you for being "kind alike to all" and "steadfastly loving one another." There is something beautiful about having a bond of unconditional love embedded into your sisterhood. I have met some of my absolute best friends through this sisterhood, and I can't imagine not having you in my life. Thank you for loving, supporting, and uplifting me and for sustaining our bond for years and decades. Each of you embody the love, power, and support that our founders instilled in our sorority from the beginning. Thank you for always being part of my story.

To my Wake Forest Crew: There is something special about the love and friendship you build through undergraduate. To those of you who walked me through the aftermath of my trauma, who stood by my side when I thought I was going to break in half, who to this day have been my rock, my sustenance, and my hope: thank you. Thank you for never letting me go and for standing me up when I didn't even have the strength to stand on my own. You have brought me the strength and foundation I so desperately needed when I was so hopelessly broken. Thank you all for continuing to be strength, light, and support in my life; for always letting me be part of your journeys; and for being such a special part of mine.

To my Pensacola crew: When you move to a new area, there is always something very special about developing your first new friendships and mentors. I am beyond grateful for the special bond I have with each of you. From vacations together to weekly wine dates to impromptu gatherings at my house to vent, share food and drinks, and just laugh, the unconditional love I have received from each of you has helped me grow into a woman who is able to be vulnerable and OK with not always being OK.

To my Magnolia Crew, my Ride Society Crew, my Deshi Crew, my Studer Community Institute Crew, and my Legacy House Crew: Thank you for the ability to release my stress, my day, and just the burdens that we all deal with in life. I know that, no matter what, I can always come here to lay down what is deep in my heart and replace it with a refreshed and renewed perspective that helps me move forward in the most positive and uplifting direction.

To my road warriors and mentors: Thank you for giving me a space to share my fears and uncertainties. Thank you for accepting those fears and uncertainties and sharing your stories to help me understand the impact of each moment in our lives and how each moment will bring us to a greater purpose. Thank you for being constantly available for all of my questions and for never losing patience, not just in answering my questions but in providing me with the resources needed to continue to grow to the next phase in my life. Thank you for your support and your love, for continuing to be part of my story, and for teaching me that my voice is important and my story deserves to be shared.

To my perfectly phenomenal editor, Mary Ward Menke: You saw my vision and shared my excitement about what we could do together. You didn't just believe in my story, you believed in the power it could have with so many people. Your insights, your recommendations, and your honesty have made this book the purposeful, impactful, fearlessly made story that it is, and it wouldn't be without you.

To Indigo River Publishing: Thank you for believing in me and my story. Thank you for wanting this story to be told and wanting others to see the vision that we had for this book and the impact we know it will have. Thank you for the platform to share my story.

Lastly, but absolutely not least, to you reading this book: Thank you for connecting and engaging with my story. We were all meant to live this life together, and my hope for you is that this story helps you feel like you have a partner along your journey.

About the Author

Kristie Tobias possesses unstoppable resilience, infectious enthusiasm, and a keen ability to connect, engage, and build relationships with everyone from CEOs of Fortune 500 companies to stay-at-home moms and dads who are CEOs of their own homes, from entrepreneurs to anyone just striving to survive *and* thrive in this sometimes messy and chaotic life.

Kristie has spent over a decade sharing her struggles with PTSD to small, intimate audiences of ten to twenty people as well as to large-scale international audiences of thousands. She believes that everyone deserves to have a voice, and she is here to support and walk alongside those who don't always feel as if their voices have been heard.

For more information, visit Kristie's website, www.fearlesslymadeyou.com, or friend her on any social media platform: on LinkedIn and Facebook under "Kristie Tobias," and on Instagram under @ktobias85.